S auces

Michel Roux

Sauces

Sweet and savoury, classic and new

TRANSLATED AND
EDITED BY KATE WHITEMAN

PHOTOGRAPHS BY
MARTIN BRIGDALE

QUADRILLE PUBLISHING

DEDICATION

The dedication of my newborn offspring *Sauces* needed only
a moment's reflection. Given that so few people have mastered this highly
important subject, I dedicate my 'baby' to young cooks all over the world
in the hope that this book will help them to discover, master and further
develop the wonderful, exhilarating world of sauces.

ACKNOWLEDGEMENTS

My thanks go to the following people for their
invaluable contributions to this book: my son Alain Roux, first sous-chef at
The Waterside Inn, who tested all the recipes and prepared them for photography;
Martin Brigdale, whose superb photos brought them to life and Helen Trent who styled
them; Mary Evans for her artistic vision and her patience in tolerating my own artistic
temperament; Paul Welti for his excellent work on the design; Kate Whiteman, who
never fails to understand what I want to say even when I have forgotten to write all
the words; Claude Grant, who typed the manuscript day and night and cheerfully
coped with my illegible writing and impossible deadlines; and my wife Robyn,
who nurtures me through the creative process and continues
to put up with my little ways.

First published in 1996
by Quadrille Publishing Limited
9 Irving Street
London WC2H 7AT

Text copyright © Michel Roux 1996
Photography copyright © Martin Brigdale 1996
Design and layout © Quadrille Publishing Ltd 1996

Art director: Mary Evans
Design: Paul Welti
Publishing director: Anne Furniss
Project editor and translator: Kate Whiteman
Styling: Helen Trent
Production: Vincent Smith

British Library Cataloguing in Publication Data
A catalogue record for this book is available from the British Library
ISBN I 899988 21 I

Printed and bound in Italy

TITLE PAGE:
ROAST DUCK WITH PEACH SAUCE

Contents

About Sauces

In my imagination, I have always envisaged the craft of cooking and all its disciplines as an ancient, vigorous and sprouting genealogical tree, whose main branches draw their life-giving sustenance from the sap in the trunk. From there, innumerable roots emanate, one of the oldest and most important, dating from time immemorial, being that of 'sauces'.

The great sauces

The great classics have been around for centuries. Noble, powerful, aristocratic and elegant, they form part of our heritage. These are sauces fit for feast days and special occasions.

The lesser sauces

There are multitudes of these, suitable for any occasion and every day. They can be prepared in a matter of moments, with very little effort, to complement a piece of meat or fish or a dish of pasta.

Modern sauces

These are the newcomers, quick and easy to prepare. They are very light, with fewer calories and are kind to the digestion. They are particularly appropriate for salads, *crudités*, vegetables and desserts.

The basic elements

All sauces, however simple or complex, should be based on good quality ingredients. Aromatics, fresh herbs, spices, wines, alcohol, stocks and *fumets* – all must be chosen with the utmost care.

The burman

A sauce-maker is like a barman mixing cocktails. It is vital to get the proportions precisely right. Ingredients with a very strong flavour, like certain pungent spices, herbs and alcohol, should be used in moderation.

The cook as alchemist

A pinch of this, a pinch of that – the creative process is bewitching. A flame licks up from the pan containing the bubbling, steaming potion, illuminating the sagacious face of the 'saucerer'. He inhales the fumes laden with the first aromas. His imagination is fired as he conjures up the magic of his sauce.

My sauces

From the age of fourteen, during my apprenticeship to a pâtissier, followed by many years in professional kitchens, I learnt the secret of sauces, from the chefs with whom I worked. Later, I developed them to suit my own palate and created original new sauces to complement my dishes.

There are sauces to suit every season, every taste, every occasion and the time available for their preparation. My objective when making a sauce, be it savoury or sweet, is to provide the perfect accompaniment to a dish and to elevate it to gastronomic perfection – but never to dominate it.

In the course of a year at The Waterside Inn, I prepare hundreds of different sauces – modern, classic, light or unctuous, depending on the dish they are to accompany. Those in this book are among my favourites. They are creative and diverse, enormously enjoyable and perfectly accessible to the home cook.

Cooking a sauce intoxicates the senses of smell, taste and sight. The visual and odiferous pleasures it offers in its final cooking stages will tempt you to dream and discover the wonderful world of sauces.

The photographs

The exceptional technical quality of the photography allows me to guide you through every process of sauce-making, vividly bringing to life the crucial stages. Together, we shall develop your talents as a sauce-maker.

Practical Advice

Choosing and flavouring sauces

MENU PLANNING: Serve only one 'grand' sauce at a meal and keep the others light and simple.

Do not serve a powerful, full-bodied sauce at the beginning of a meal.

Try to avoid serving sauces of the same colour and texture, or with a similar base, such as wine or liqueurs. Do not make all the sauces at the same meal too classic or too modern. Your guests will appreciate a judicious balance.

SEASONAL PRODUCE: In the same way that you would choose the finest seasonal ingredients for a finished dish, make your sauces with the best seasonal produce. The end result will be full of flavour and all the more delicious.

SEASONING: Never add too much salt to a sauce before it has reached the desired consistency and taste. Add pepper only just before serving to retain its flavour and zip.

CURRY POWDER: Add a pinch of curry powder to foaming melted butter to enhance the flavours of steamed fish, white meats and vegetables.

GARLIC: Always halve garlic cloves lengthways and remove the green shoot, which can be indigestible.

MUSHROOMS: Their wild, musky aroma of forest bark and damp earth adds a special something to many sauces. It is better to wipe fresh mushrooms clean than to wash them, as they absorb water and lose their flavour. Chop or finely slice them and add to the sauce during cooking. Some varieties, such as button or white cultivated mushrooms, tend to lack flavour, so be generous with these. Others, such as shiitake, have quite an aggressive flavour and should be used

TO CRUSH GARLIC, PUT THE PEELED CLOVES IN A MORTAR WITH A GOOD PINCH OF COARSE SALT

CRUSH THE GARLIC TO A PASTE WITH A PESTLE

sparingly. Dried mushrooms are a good substitute for fresh (soak them first), but for the ultimate pleasure, black or white truffles can be added to numerous sauces a few minutes before serving.

SAFFRON: To obtain the maximum flavour when using saffron threads, pound them in a mortar or crush them with your fingertips into the palm of your hand, then infuse them in a little warm water.

SHELLFISH COOKING JUICES: Keep the cooking juices from oysters, mussels, clams etc. As soon as possible after cooking the molluscs, add a small amount to fish sauces to reinforce their flavour and make them more complex.

SHALLOTS: Shallots become bitter after chopping, so rinse them under cold water before using in a sauce.

VEGETABLE ESSENCES: These are used to lighten a sauce which is over-rich, powerful or too thick, or to add a more aromatic flavour to a sauce or vegetable *court-bouillon*. They can also be served separately in a ramekin to accompany steamed fish, or stirred warm into a vinaigrette to serve with vegetables or shellfish.

Vegetable essences can be made with almost any kind of vegetables. Chop them finely or coarsely, depending on their structure, place in a pan with a very small amount of liquid (water or chicken stock). Cover and cook until tender, then strain through a fine-mesh conical sieve and keep in a small airtight jar.

VINEGAR AND LEMON: A few drops of vinegar or lemon juice added to a characterless sauce just before serving will pep up the taste.

Preparing, keeping and freezing sauces

PREPARATION TIME: The preparation times given in this book are based on ingredients which have already been weighed out and prepared as indicated in the ingredients list. They do not include the time taken to peel, chop, slice or blanch vegetables or bones, soften butter etc, or any necessary cooling time.

COOKING TIMES: The timings given for cooking and reducing sauces are intended only as guidelines, since the degree of heat will vary depending on your hob and the type of saucepan used. The only infallible way to ensure that a sauce has reached the desired consistency is to check it on the back of a spoon.

DEGREASING: The easiest way to degrease a stock is to leave it to cool completely at room temperature, then refrigerate it. The fat will solidify on the surface and can be carefully lifted off with a large spoon.

DEGLAZING: Liquid such as wine or stock is heated with the cooking juices and sediment left in the pan after roasting or pan-frying to make a sauce or gravy. Remove most of the fat and grease from the pan before adding the liquid.

STRAINING: Thin sauces can be passed straight through a conical sieve. Thicker sauces should be pushed through the sieve by pressing with the back of a ladle or twisting a small whisk.

HOT EMULSION SAUCES: These sauces do not like to be kept waiting. To enjoy them at their delicate best, make them at the last possible moment and serve immediately.

KEEPING SAUCES WARM: A bain-marie is best for this. Use a saucepan large enough to hold the pan or bowl containing the sauce, and fill it with hot water.

Dot flakes of butter over the surface of white sauces to prevent a skin from forming. Sauces which need a liaison or 'smoothing' with butter should be kept in the bain-marie, and the liaison or butter added at the moment of serving.

FREEZING: All stocks and *fumets* freeze well. Store them in small airtight freezer containers then, whenever you need some, just tip the frozen block of stock into a saucepan and heat gently.

A CLASSIC BOUQUET GARNI
CONSISTS OF A SPRIG OF
THYME, A BAY LEAF,
PARSLEY STALKS AND A
LEEK LEAF

WRAP THE HERBS IN THE
LEEK LEAF AND TIE UP
THE BOUQUET GARNI
WITH STRING

Herbs and spices

This subject deserves an entire encyclopaedia to do it justice instead of just a few lines. But since this is a book about sauces, I shall mention only those herbs and spices which are familiar to me and which I use to flavour and enhance my own cooking.

In Bray, I have created a herb garden on the banks of the Thames. Every day in the summer months, I painstakingly and parsimoniously pick the numerous different herbs I need for my sauces and salads. Freshness is a vital factor in the success of a sauce and my herb garden is my trump card.

If you use dried herbs, keep them in airtight jars in a cool, dark place. Spices lose their colour and flavour if they are kept too long; you should throw away any open ones after 3 – 6 months because they will add nothing to your sauces, and may even spoil them.

The golden rules for using herbs and spices are:
* Small quantities but good quality.
* Do not mix contradictory and powerful flavours.
If you obey these rules, you will discover a wonderful world of flavours – subtle, complex, musky, fresh, spicy and delectable.

Fines herbes are a mixture of fresh herbs in equal quantities: chervil, chives, parsley and tarragon. They should be snipped, not chopped, preferably only a short time before using so that they retain the maximum flavour and do not become bitter.

The most popular culinary herbs are: basil, bay leaf, chervil, chives, fresh coriander, dill, fennel, garlic, horseradish, lavender, lemon grass, lemon verbena, lovage, marjoram, mint, oregano, flat or curly parsley, rosemary, sage, savory, sorrel, tarragon and thyme.

The most popular spices are: caraway, cardamom, cayenne, cinnamon, cloves, coriander seeds, cumin, curry, five-spice, ginger, juniper, mace, nutmeg, black, green, white and pink pepper, paprika, pimento, poppy seeds, saffron and star anise.

Capers are also a popular ingredient, as is vanilla, the most famous of all aromatics for sweet sauces.

TO FLAVOUR A SAUCE
WITH PEPPERCORNS,
CRUSH THEM AND
PLACE ON A PIECE OF
MUSLIN

FOLD UP THE EDGES
TO MAKE A PURSE
AND TIE WITH
STRING

Dairy products

These play an extremely important part in sauce-making.

UNSALTED BUTTER: The finest of all dairy products. It is natural and healthy and practically indispensable in the kitchen. Its delicate taste and different complexities vary according to its provenance and origins. It adds the finishing touch to many of my sauces, but I always use it in moderation. I use only unsalted butter in my cooking. This is essential for making clarified butter and desirable for all sauces.

At The Waterside Inn, after many blind tastings, the butter I have chosen for the table and for my *beurres blancs* and sauces is the *appellation contrôlée* Echiré from the Deux-Sèvres. Its quality and value place it among the very best French butters.

When either unsalted and salted butter is melted, its components separate into 15 – 20% water, 4% protein, and the balance is butterfat.

DOUBLE CREAM: This tolerates heat extremely well during cooking and can even be reduced by boiling. It is often used as a liaison, but above all it makes sauces creamy and velvety. It comes in both full and reduced-fat versions.

CRÈME FRAÎCHE: This can be heated to not more than 80°C, after which it will separate. To use it in a hot sauce, whisk it into the sauce off the heat, without further cooking. This slightly acidulated cream is light and refreshing and is delicious added to most cold sauces.

FROMAGE BLANC: This is the champion of low calorie sauces; you can even buy a virtually fat-free version. It is perfect for summer sauces, but its neutral taste demands the addition of spices, herbs etc.

YOGHURT: I use tiny quantities of yoghurt to finish certain fish sauces in order to add a touch of acidity. I use it more often in quite a few of my low-calorie summer vinaigrettes and in some fruit coulis, where it develops a hint of acidity and freshness.

HARD CHEESES: The most important and best are parmesan, gruyère, emmenthal and cheddar. I always buy medium-matured farmhouse cheeses, which have a full, sublime flavour. These cheeses are usually used freshly-grated to finish a sauce. It takes a few minutes after they have been added for their savour to develop, so you should use them judiciously and parsimoniously at first, checking their development before adding more to the sauce.

Do not use cheap, poor quality cheese, which can ruin a sauce by tasting rancid, soapy or too salty.

ROQUEFORT: My noble Lord Roquefort will acquire star status in a salad dressing, a cold sauce for *crudités* and certain hot sauces. I adore roquefort. Used in moderation, it creates an explosion of different savours in a sauce. Bleu d'Auvergne and Fourme d'Ambert make adequate substitutes, but cannot equal the real thing.

Sauce-making equipment

ALL YOU NEED TO MAKE PERFECT SAUCES

OPPOSITE PAGE:

1. SAUCEPAN WITH SLOPING SIDES,
   SAUCEPAN, STOCK POT
2. STRAIGHT-SIDED SAUCEPANS, BAIN-MARIE
3. LARGE SPOON, LADLE, SKIMMER, SLOTTED
   SPOON, FINE STRAINER
4. WEIGHING SCALES, MEASURING JUG,
   COOKING THERMOMETER
5. PESTLE AND MORTAR
6. STRAINER, WIRE-MESH AND RIGID
   CONICAL SIEVES
7. BLENDER GOBLET, HAND-HELD BLENDER
8. ZESTER, MANDOLINE
9. ASSORTED BASINS AND BOWLS

THIS PAGE, LEFT TO RIGHT:

BALLOON WHISK
RUBBER AND WOODEN SPATULAS,
    WOODEN SPOON
WOODEN FOOD PUSHER, DRUM SIEVE

All this equipment can be obtained from M.O.R.A
(Matérial Outillage Rationnel pour l'Alimentation),
13 rue Montmartre, 75001 Paris.
Tel: 45 08 19 24
Fax: 45 08 49 05

C H A P T E R   1

These are indispensable to the preparation of the great classic sauces and play a significant part in many others. Given their importance, they should be prepared with great care.

Stocks are the very foundation of sauces; on their quality depends the success of your sauces and your mastery of sauce-making.

S t o c k s

THE GOLDEN RULES OF STOCK-MAKING

* All the ingredients — meat, poultry or fish bones, aromatics, vegetables, wines etc. — must be extremely fresh and of the highest quality.

* Equally important — do not drown the stock at the outset by adding too much water to the ingredients; it will make it tasteless and watery. Better to add too little water than too much; if necessary you can always add more cold water during cooking.

* Always add **cold** *water to a stock. Hot water will make it cloudy and you will lose the desired crystal clarity.*

* Cooking a stock for longer does not make it better — quite the reverse. Long cooking can actually be detrimental, since the stock becomes heavy and loses its savour. Follow the cooking times in the recipes precisely; only veal stock needs several hours cooking.

* For a double depth of flavour, cook the stock twice, using cold water the first time, and the cooled batch of stock the second time.

In essence, stocks are embryonic sauces, which must be carefully nurtured and titivated. They should be cooked at a simmer and never allowed to boil, and must be skimmed and degreased at regular intervals to remove all impurities. Finally, they must be strained gently and delicately through a wire-mesh conical sieve, taking care not to cloud their clarity.

Veal Stock

Fond de veau

Veal stock forms the base for almost all brown sauces, and is often used in fish sauces as well.

Makes 1 litre
PREPARATION TIME: 30 MINUTES
COOKING TIME: ABOUT 3 HOURS

Ingredients:
1.5KG VEAL BONES, CHOPPED
1/2 CALF'S FOOT, SPLIT LENGTHWAYS, CHOPPED AND BLANCHED
200G CARROTS, CUT INTO ROUNDS
100G ONION, COARSELY CHOPPED
250ML DRY WHITE WINE
1 CELERY STALK, THINLY SLICED
6 TOMATOES, PEELED, DESEEDED AND CHOPPED
150G BUTTON MUSHROOMS, THINLY SLICED
2 GARLIC CLOVES
1 BOUQUET GARNI (PAGE 10), INCLUDING A SPRIG OF TARRAGON

Preheat the oven to 220°C/425°F/gas mark 7. Put the veal bones and calf's foot in a roasting pan and brown in the oven, turning them from time to time with a slotted spoon. When they have browned, add the carrots and onions, mix together and cook for another 5 minutes. Using the slotted spoon, transfer all the contents of the roasting pan to a large saucepan or casserole. Pour off the fat from the roasting pan and deglaze with the white wine, scraping up all the sediment. Set over high heat and reduce by half, then pour the wine into the saucepan. Add 3L cold water and bring to the boil over high heat. As soon as the liquid boils, reduce the heat so that the surface is barely trembling. Simmer for 10 minutes, then skim well and add all the other ingredients.

Simmer the stock, uncovered, for 2 1/2 hours, skimming as necessary. Strain through a fine-mesh conical sieve into a bowl and cool over ice (see page 22).

DEMI-GLACE OR GLACE: Reduce the strained stock by one-third to make a *demi-glace*; reduce by half for a *glace*. These *glaces* enhance sauces, adding moistness and a fuller flavour. But they cannot add finesse and subtlety, since the lengthy cooking time involved destroys some of their delicate flavour and aroma.

PUT THE BONES IN THE ROASTING PAN

BROWN THE BONES, CARROTS AND ONIONS

RIGHT: ADD THE VEGETABLES AND AROMATICS

INSET: STRAIN THE STOCK AND COOL IT OVER A BOWL OF ICE

DEGLAZE THE PAN WITH THE WINE

SKIM THE SURFACE OF THE STOCK

Chicken Stock

Fond de volaille

I sometimes add half a knuckle of veal when preparing this stock, which makes it extra rich and unctuous.

Makes about 1.5 litres
PREPARATION TIME: 15 MINUTES
COOKING TIME: ABOUT 1 3/4 HOURS

Ingredients:
1 BOILING FOWL, WEIGHING 1.5KG, OR AN EQUAL
WEIGHT OF CHICKEN CARCASSES OR WINGS,
BLANCHED AND REFRESHED
200G CARROTS, CUT INTO CHUNKS
WHITE PART OF 2 LEEKS, CUT INTO CHUNKS
1 CELERY STALK, COARSELY CHOPPED
1 ONION, STUDDED WITH 2 CLOVES
150G BUTTON MUSHROOMS, THINLY SLICED
1 BOUQUET GARNI (PAGE 10)

Put the chicken or carcasses in a saucepan and cover with 2.5L cold water. Bring to the boil over high heat, then immediately lower the heat and keep at a simmer. After 5 minutes, skim the surface and add all the other ingredients. Cook gently for $1^{1}/_2$ hours, without boiling, skimming whenever necessary.

Strain the stock through a wire-mesh conical sieve and cool it as quickly as possible (see page 22).

Lamb Stock

Fond d'agneau

This lamb stock is light in both flavour and appearance. I use it for deglazing in many roast or pan-fried lamb recipes, such as a navarin. It can form the basis for a sauce, in which case I would flavour it with curry, star anise, mint or saffron etc to complement the dish. For a wonderful taste of spring, I sometimes use the stock to moisten a cous-cous garnished with tender young vegetables.

Makes 1 litre
PREPARATION TIME: 30 MINUTES
COOKING TIME: ABOUT 2 HOURS

Ingredients:
1.5KG SCRAG END, BREAST OR LOWER BEST END OF
LAMB, SKIN AND FAT REMOVED, CUT INTO PIECES
150G CARROTS, CUT INTO ROUNDS
100G ONIONS, COARSELY CHOPPED
250ML DRY WHITE WINE
4 TOMATOES, PEELED, DESEEDED AND CHOPPED
2 GARLIC CLOVES
1 BOUQUET GARNI (PAGE 10), INCLUDING 2 SPRIGS
OF TARRAGON AND A CELERY STALK
6 WHITE PEPPERCORNS, CRUSHED

Preheat the oven to 220°C/425°F/gas mark 7. Put the pieces of lamb in a roasting pan and brown in the hot oven, turning them over from time to time with a slotted spoon. When the lamb has coloured, add the carrots and onions, mix together and cook for another 5 minutes. Still using the slotted spoon, transfer all the contents of the roasting pan to a large saucepan or casserole. Pour off the fat from the roasting pan, deglaze with the white wine and reduce by half. Pour the reduced wine into the saucepan, add 2.5L cold water and bring to the boil over high heat. As soon as the liquid boils, reduce the heat so that the surface is barely trembling. Simmer for 10 minutes, then skim the surface and add all the other ingredients.

Simmer, uncovered, for $1^{1}/_2$ hours, skimming the surface as necessary. Strain the stock through a fine-mesh conical sieve into a bowl and cool it as quickly as possible (see page 22).

Game Stock

Fond de gibier

This stock makes the perfect sauce for pan-fried noisettes of venison. Deglaze the pan with port, add a teaspoon of redcurrant jelly, then the game stock. Whisk in a knob of butter and season to taste. Delicious!

Makes 1.5 litres
PREPARATION TIME: 30 MINUTES
COOKING TIME: 2¼ HOURS

Ingredients:
3 TBSP GROUNDNUT OIL
2 KG FURRED OR FEATHERED GAME TRIMMINGS,
CARCASSES, NECKS, WINGS ETC, CUT INTO PIECES
150G CARROTS, CUT INTO ROUNDS
150G ONIONS, COARSELY CHOPPED
½ HEAD OF GARLIC, HALVED WIDTHWAYS
500ML RED WINE (PREFERABLY CÔTES DU RHÔNE)
500ML VEAL STOCK (PAGE 16)
8 JUNIPER BERRIES, CRUSHED
8 CORIANDER SEEDS, CRUSHED
1 BOUQUET GARNI (PAGE 10), INCLUDING 2 SAGE
LEAVES AND A CELERY STALK

Preheat the oven to 220°C/425°F/gas mark 7. Heat the oil in a roasting pan, then put in the game carcasses or trimmings and brown in the hot oven, turning them from time to time with a slotted spoon. When the meat has browned, add the carrots, onions and garlic, mix together and cook for another 5 minutes. With the slotted spoon, transfer all the contents of the roasting pan to a large saucepan or casserole. Pour off the fat from the roasting pan and deglaze with the red wine. Set over high heat and reduce the wine by half, then pour it into the saucepan. Add 2 L cold water and bring to the boil over high heat. As soon as the liquid boils, reduce the heat so that the surface barely trembles. Simmer for 10 minutes, then skim well and add all the other ingredients.

Simmer the stock, uncovered, for 2 hours, skimming the surface as necessary. Strain it through a fine-mesh conical sieve into a bowl and cool as quickly as possible (see page 22).

Once the stock has been strained, you can reduce it by one-third to give it more body. Like all stocks, it will keep well for several days in the fridge, or for three or four months in the freezer.

Fish
Stock or Fumet

Fumet de poisson

Fish stock can be used as the base for an aspic to serve with cold fish. Just add a few gelatine leaves and season with salt and pepper before the gelatine sets. If you intend to use the stock for a red wine sauce, substitute red wine for the white when making the stock.

SKIM THE SURFACE OF
THE STOCK

Makes 2 litres
PREPARATION TIME: 20 MINUTES
COOKING TIME: ABOUT 30 MINUTES

Ingredients:
1.5KG BONES AND TRIMMINGS OF WHITE FISH (EG SOLE, TURBOT, BRILL, WHITING), CUT INTO PIECES
50G BUTTER
WHITE OF 2 LEEKS, THINLY SLICED
75G ONIONS, THINLY SLICED
75G BUTTON MUSHROOMS, THINLY SLICED
200ML DRY WHITE WINE
1 BOUQUET GARNI (PAGE 10)
2 SLICES OF LEMON
8 WHITE PEPPERCORNS, CRUSHED AND WRAPPED IN A PIECE OF MUSLIN (PAGE 11)

Rinse the fish bones and trimmings under cold running water, then drain (1). In a saucepan, melt the butter and sweat the vegetables over low heat for a few minutes. Add the fish bones and trimmings (2), bubble gently for a few moments, then pour in the wine (3). Cook until it has evaporated by two-thirds, then add 2.5L cold water (4). Bring to the boil, lower the heat, skim the surface and add the bouquet garni and lemon. Simmer very gently for 25 minutes, skimming as necessary. 10 minutes before the end of cooking, add the muslin-wrapped peppercorns.

Gently ladle the stock through a fine-mesh conical sieve and cool it as quickly as possible (see page 22).

FISH VELOUTÉ: For an excellent fish *velouté*, add 60g white roux (page 33) per litre of stock and cook for 20 minutes.

ADD THE MUSLIN-WRAPPED
PEPPERCORNS

STRAIN THE STOCK
THROUGH A FINE-MESH
CONICAL SIEVE

Vegetable Stock or Nage

Court-bouillon de légumes ou Nage

Nages are light aromatic poaching stocks, and I like to add a hint of accidity to mine, hence the vinegar. I don't, however, use vinegar in my classic vegetable stock. You can substitute or add your own choice of seasonal vegetables, varying the stock with nice ripe tomatoes in summer, a few wild mushrooms in autumn (chanterelles add a particularly fine aroma), and so on.

Makes 1.5 litres
PREPARATION TIME: 15 MINUTES
COOKING TIME: 45 MINUTES

Ingredients:
300G CARROTS, CUT INTO ROUNDS
WHITE PART OF 2 LEEKS, THINLY SLICED
100G CELERY STALKS, THINLY SLICED
50G BULB FENNEL, VERY THINLY SLICED
150G SHALLOTS, THINLY SLICED
100G ONION, THINLY SLICED
2 UNPEELED GARLIC CLOVES
1 BOUQUET GARNI (PAGE 10)
250ML DRY WHITE WINE
2L WATER
10 WHITE PEPPERCORNS, CRUSHED AND WRAPPED
IN MUSLIN (PAGE 10)
3 TBSP WHITE WINE VINEGAR (ONLY FOR A *NAGE*)

Put all the ingredients except the peppercorns in a saucepan. Bring to the boil over high heat, then cook at a bare simmer for 45 minutes, skimming as necessary. After 35 minutes, add the muslin-wrapped peppercorns. Strain through a fine-mesh conical sieve into a bowl and cool as quickly as possible (see below).

COOLING AND FREEZING STOCKS
In the restaurant I cool my strained stocks very rapidly using a blast freezer to prevent the spread of bacteria. At home, I fill a container with ice cubes and plunge in the pan or bowl of boiling stock, which cools quite quickly. As soon as the stock is cold, I transfer it to airtight containers, keeping what I need in the fridge and freezing the rest. All stocks can be kept in the fridge for several days, or for several weeks in the freezer.

PUT THE INGREDIENTS
INTO THE SAUCEPAN

SKIM THE SURFACE OF
THE STOCK

RIGHT: STRAIN THE STOCK
AND COOL IT QUICKLY
OVER A BOWL OF ICE

Cooked Marinade

Marinade ordinaire cuite

Large pieces of meat or game can be left in the cold marinade for one to three days; smaller pieces should be marinated for one or two hours. If you plan to serve the meat the same day, it can be placed in the marinade while this is still warm. Always use tongs or a fork to turn the meat in the marinade, never your fingers, which will spoil it.

The addition of a small amount of marinade to a game sauce will reinforce its structure and flavour.

Makes 1.5 litres
(Sufficient for a large piece of meat)
PREPARATION TIME: ABOUT 10 MINUTES
COOKING TIME: ABOUT 25 MINUTES

Ingredients:
20G BUTTER
2 CARROTS, CUT INTO ROUNDS
2 ONIONS, ROUGHLY CHOPPED
1 CELERY STALK, THINLY SLICED
1L RED WINE (PREFERABLY CÔTES DU RHÔNE)
100ML RED WINE VINEGAR
750ML WATER
1 BOUQUET GARNI (PAGE 10), INCLUDING A SPRIG
OF ROSEMARY
1/2 HEAD OF GARLIC, HALVED WIDTHWAYS
2 CLOVES
A PINCH OF CRUSHED PEPPERCORNS

In a saucepan, melt the butter and sweat the vegetables for a few minutes. Add all the other ingredients and bring to the boil over high heat. Immediately lower the heat and cook gently for 20 minutes, skimming the surface whenever necessary. Unless you are going to serve the meat the same day, cool the marinade completely before using it.

The choice of a liaison depends entirely on personal taste and the time available to make the sauce. It is like the gradation between a steak cooked bleu and one which is very well done; the range in between is enormous.

In this chapter, I aim to guide you through the different methods and types of liaison, explaining how to use them and which method best suits which type of sauce — but there are no rigid rules.

Liaisons &
Instant Sauces

Although very thick sauces are no longer fashionable, there is no need to go too far in the other direction; any excess is ridiculous. We have all suffered ultra-light offerings from contemporary chefs which are more like badly-seasoned bouillons than sauces. They remind me of the days of nouvelle cuisine, when you needed a magnifying glass to find the chef's minuscule creation on a huge plate. A sauce is not a glass of water; its consistency is as important as its taste and it is vital to strike a happy balance.

The popularity of the sauce spoon spread in the 1960s and enabled us easily and elegantly to sup up and enjoy the more liquid, lighter, foamy sauces which are better suited to today's tastes.

It is worth mentioning the very simplest liaisons which require no recipe, such as a few caramelized onions, crushed into a sauce with a fork, or a little roasted carrot or potato given the same treatment. Garlic or shallots baked in their skins on a bed of coarse salt make a lovely thickener for lamb gravy or sauce from a pot-roasted chicken.

Also included in this chapter are some very quick recipes which require virtually no cooking. You could devise many others using the same simple principles.

THICKENING AND LIGHTENING
A SAUCE WITH BUTTER

Liaison techniques

Breadcrumbs

Breadcrumbs are used as a thickening agent for rustic, flavourful sauces. In country cooking, they are used to thicken the broth from a pot-au-feu or the pan juices from a roast. These are my favourite sauces when I cook at my house in Gassin in Provence.

FRESH BREADCRUMBS:
Crumble them into the warm sauce and cook very gently for about 20 minutes, whisking from time to time. When the sauce reaches the desired consistency, serve it just as it is, or pass it through a fine conical strainer.

TOASTED BREADCRUMBS:
Crumble them into a bowl, drizzle in a little olive oil and, if you like, a small quantity of ground almonds. Mix thoroughly with a fork. Add the mixture to your warm sauce and bring to the boil over low heat. Bubble gently for 5-10 minutes until the sauce has thickened.

Egg yolks

Sauces bound with egg yolks have a velvety texture and delicate colour. They always remind me of the creamy blanquette de veau which my mother prepared at home when I was a child.

In a bowl, break up the egg yolks with a very little barely tepid liquid: use milk, wine, chicken stock etc. depending on the sauce. Off the heat, pour the yolks into the almost boiling sauce, stirring continuously with a wooden spoon. Over low heat, reheat the sauce, stirring constantly until it lightly coats the back of the spoon. It is essential not to let the sauce boil, or it will separate. As soon as it has thickened, pass it through a fine conical strainer into a clean saucepan and keep warm.

Cornflour, rice flour and arrowroot

These vegetable thickeners are quick and easy to use, need no special skill, and are ideal when you need a sauce in a hurry. In a bowl, dissolve the thickening agent in a little cold liquid — water, milk or wine — and pour into the boiling sauce. Simmer for about 10 minutes; the sauce will thicken almost instantaneously.

Double cream

Cream-thickened sauces are often used for fish, poultry, veloutés and certain soups. They add a velvet-smooth quality, which I love.

Always use double cream. You will need about 10-20% cream in proportion to the quantity of sauce. Boil the cream for a few minutes, then stir it into the boiling sauce.

The consistency, taste and properties of double cream vary from country to country. For example, in Britain, it is soft and delicate and can be stirred directly into the sauce and boiled without separating. In France crème fraîche is slightly acidulated and cannot easily be added uncooked to a sauce, or it will split.

SWIRL THE BUTTER INTO A SAUCE, A LITTLE
AT A TIME, TO LIGHTEN AND THICKEN IT

Blood

Blood is mainly used as a thickener for sauces for game, such as venison and wild boar, or in the sauce for canard au sang. *I use a touch in the red wine sauce which I often serve with duck at The Waterside Inn, and also in* civet of hare, *which is a favourite dish of mine.*

Blood used for cooking almost always comes from pigs, rabbit or poultry (usually chicken). It is important that it does not coagulate; a few drops of vinegar added as soon as you obtain the blood will prevent this.

Allow about 150ml blood for 1 litre of sauce, or a little more if you want a thicker sauce.

Take the almost boiling sauce off the heat and add the blood, stirring continuously with a wooden spatula. Replace the pan over medium heat and cook the sauce until it thickens, stirring all the time. As soon as the surface begins to tremble, stop the cooking and immediately pass the sauce through a fine conical strainer into another pan. Keep it warm and serve it as soon as possible.

Lightening and thickening with butter

Incorporating butter into a sauce improves it in five important ways, making it lighter, smoother, glossier, thicker and mellower. Once ready, these delicate sauces must not be allowed to boil and should be served as soon as possible. The butter should be well-chilled, almost frozen. Take the boiling sauce off the heat and incorporate small pieces of butter (5-10g), one at a time. Either use a balloon whisk or hold the pan handle firmly and swirl or shake the pan from side to side, until all the butter is incorporated.

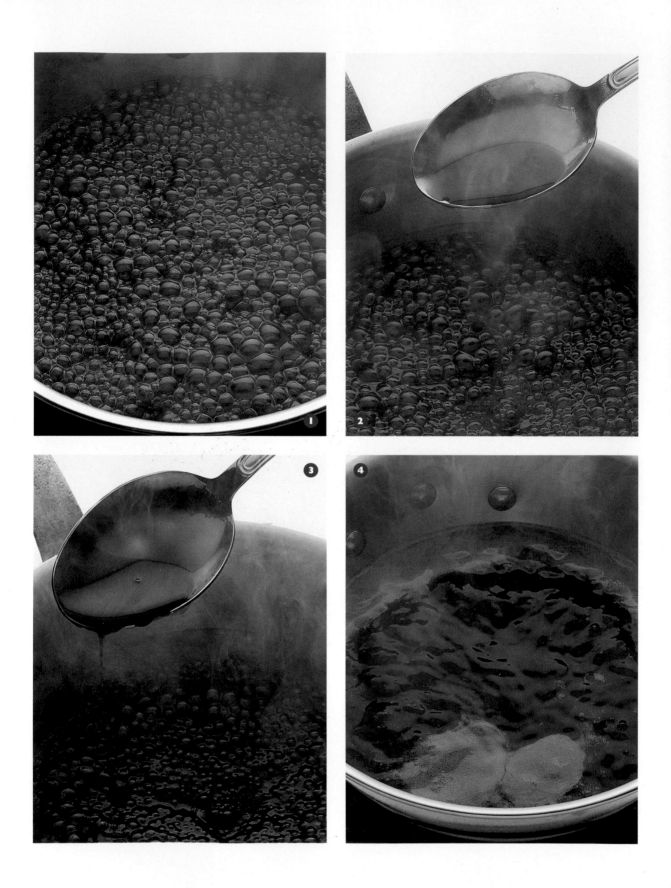

Reduction

You should be able to judge by eye when a sauce has reached the desired consistency by reduction, but it is helpful to use the back of a spoon to gauge the precise thickness. Let the sauce cool slightly before running your finger down the spoon.

Reduce the sauce over high heat to obtain the required consistency — a light juice (1), slightly syrupy (2), syrupy (3) or the very thick, rich demi-glace (6). As the sauce reduces, impurities rise to the surface (4); skim off as necessary (5). Never season a reduction sauce before it reaches the desired consistency.

Using a blender

Sauces emulsified in a blender are very light and should be used immediately to retain their airy quality. They are often based on vegetable or fish stock, or beurre blanc.

Pour the finished sauce into the goblet of a blender, or use a hand blender, and whizz for 2-5 minutes, depending on how airy and mousse-like you want your sauce to be.

Beurre manié

Beurre manié is used to thicken sauces rapidly. Use only a small quantity, or the sauce will become too heavy.

It consists of two-thirds volume softened butter and one-third sifted flour, mashed together (uncooked) with a fork. Using a small whisk, incorporate small quantities of beurre manié into the sauce over high heat. The sauce will thicken immediately; let it bubble a few times, then as soon as it reaches the desired consistency, pass it through a wire-mesh conical strainer.

Clarified butter

Clarified butter is used to cook meat over a high heat without blackening it. It is also used for emulsified sauces like hollandaise and its derivatives and for making brown roux. During the clarifying process, the butter loses about 20% of its original weight.

To make about 100g clarified butter, start with 120g unsalted butter. Melt this over a very gentle heat and bring slowly to the boil. Skim off the froth from the surface. Carefully pour the liquid butter into a bowl, taking care not to include any of the milky sediment from the bottom of the pan. The clarified butter should be the colour of a light olive oil.

Clarified butter will keep in the fridge for several weeks.

SAUCES WILL FROTH UP
WHEN EMULSIFIED
WITH A HAND BLENDER,
SO MAKE SURE YOU USE
A DEEP ENOUGH
SAUCEPAN

SKIM OFF THE FROTH
FROM THE SURFACE OF
THE BUTTER

CAREFULLY POUR THE
LIQUID CLARIFIED
BUTTER INTO A BOWL

① ② ③ ④

White Roux

This roux is classically used as a thickener in all white sauces.

Makes 100g
PREPARATION TIME: 3 MINUTES
COOKING TIME: 4 MINUTES

Ingredients:
50G BUTTER
50G FLOUR, SIFTED

Melt the butter in a heavy-based saucepan (1). Off the heat, add the flour (2) and stir in with a small whisk or a wooden spoon (3), then cook over medium heat for 3 minutes, stirring continuously (4). Transfer to a bowl, cover with cling film and keep at room temperature, or store in the fridge for several days.

Blond Roux

This pale roux is used to thicken veloutés and sauces where a neutral colour is required, particularly those for lamb, veal and all poultry.

Makes 100g
PREPARATION TIME: 3 MINUTES
COOKING TIME: 6 MINUTES

Ingredients:
50G BUTTER
50G FLOUR, SIFTED

Melt the butter in a heavy-based saucepan. Take the pan off the heat and stir in the flour with a small whisk or a spatula. Cook the roux over medium heat for 5 minutes, stirring continuously, until it becomes a pale hazelnut brown (5). Transfer to a bowl, cover with cling film and keep at room temperature. The roux can be stored in the fridge for several days.

Brown Roux

This roux is used to thicken many brown sauces. The clarified butter gives the sauce a deep colour without adding any of the bitterness or unpleasant flavour of burnt butter.

Makes 100g
PREPARATION TIME: 3 MINUTES
COOKING TIME: 9 MINUTES

Ingredients:
50G CLARIFIED BUTTER (PAGE 31)
50G FLOUR, SIFTED

Heat the clarified butter in a heavy-based saucepan (6). Take the pan off the heat and stir in the flour using a small whisk or a spatula. Cook the roux over medium heat for 8 minutes, stirring continuously, until it becomes chestnut brown (7). Transfer to a bowl, cover with cling film and keep at room temperature. The roux can be stored in the fridge for several days.

Fromage Blanc Sauce with Curry

Sauce au fromage blanc au parfum de curry

Use this sauce as a dressing for a summer salad of green beans, new potatoes or crudités, or with cold cooked mussels.
You can adjust the quantity of curry slightly to suit your own taste, or even substitute 15g fresh mint, which you infuse in the milk. This version is delicious with cold pasta and a scattering of shredded mint leaves.

Serves 6
PREPARATION TIME: 3 MINUTES
COOKING TIME: 2 MINUTES

Ingredients:
100ML MILK
1 TBSP CURRY POWDER
300G FROMAGE BLANC (WHICHEVER FAT CONTENT YOU PREFER)
SALT AND FRESHLY GROUND PEPPER

In a small saucepan, bring the milk to the boil. Add the curry, simmer for 2 minutes, then leave at room temperature to cool completely. Strain the cold curry-flavoured milk through a wire-mesh sieve, then stir it into the *fromage blanc*. Season to taste with salt and pepper. The sauce is now ready to use.

Yoghurt Sauce

Sauce au yaourt

This refreshing sauce is excellent with all cold vegetables, cold pasta, fish and hard-boiled eggs. It is very quick to make.

Serves 8
PREPARATION TIME: 10 MINUTES

Ingredients:
600ML PLAIN YOGHURT
100G MAYONNAISE (SEE PAGE 109)
2 TBSP SNIPPED FRESH HERBS OF YOUR CHOICE (EG CHERVIL, PARSLEY, CHIVES, TARRAGON)
1 MEDIUM MARMANDE TOMATO, PEELED, DESEEDED AND DICED
A SMALL PINCH OF CAYENNE PEPPER, OR 4 DROPS OF TABASCO
SALT

Mix all the ingredients together and, *voilà*, your sauce is ready to serve.

Herb Butter Sauce

Beurre battu aux herbes

At The Waterside Inn, I roll boiled potatoes or small carrots in this sauce to make them savoury and shiny.

Serves 6
PREPARATION TIME: 3 MINUTES
COOKING TIME: 5 MINUTES

Ingredients:
125ML COLD WATER
A SMALL BUNCH OF EQUAL QUANTITIES OF TARRAGON AND FLAT-LEAF PARSLEY, CHOPPED
200G BUTTER, CHILLED AND DICED
JUICE OF 1/2 LEMON
SALT AND FRESHLY GROUND PEPPER

Put the water and herbs in a saucepan and bring to the boil. Over very low heat, add the butter, whisking continuously. At the last moment, add the lemon juice, season to taste with salt and pepper and pass the sauce through a wire-mesh sieve. Serve immediately.

Fishbone Sauce

Sauce à l'arête

This sauce is quick to prepare, light and full of flavour. It goes very well with poached fish or steamed scallops.

Serves 4
PREPARATION TIME: 10 MINUTES
COOKING TIME: 10 MINUTES

Ingredients:
150G BUTTER, DICED
40G SHALLOT, CHOPPED
200G WHITE FISH BONES (EG SOLE OR TURBOT),
ROUGHLY CHOPPED
100ML DRY WHITE WINE
100ML COLD WATER
1 SPRIG OF THYME
A FEW DROPS OF LEMON JUICE
SALT AND FRESHLY GROUND PEPPER

Melt 50g butter in a small saucepan. Add the shallot and fishbones, and sweat gently for 3 minutes, stirring with a wooden spoon. Pour in the wine and cook for 2 minutes. Add the water and thyme and bubble for 3 minutes, then skim the surface if necessary. Toss in the remaining butter, one piece at a time, rotating the pan and swirling it about to incorporate the butter, then add the lemon juice. Season to taste with salt and pepper and pass the sauce through a wire-mesh conical sieve. It is now ready to use.

Fresh Goat's Cheese Sauce with Rosemary

Sauce au fromage de chèvre frais et au romarin

Serve this sauce with a basket of crudités or cold dishes such as poached fish, roast or poached chicken, or with large pink shrimps or prawns.

Serves 6
PREPARATION TIME: 3 MINUTES

Ingredients:
250ML MILK (IF THE CHEESE HAS A VERY SOFT
CONSISTENCY, YOU MAY NEED ONLY 150–200ML)
30G FRESH ROSEMARY NEEDLES
300G FRESH GOAT'S CHEESE, SOFTENED WITH A
SPATULA
SALT AND FRESHLY GROUND PEPPER

In a small saucepan, bring the milk to the boil. Add the rosemary needles, cover the pan and leave to infuse until completely cold. Strain the cooled milk, whisk it into the goat's cheese and season to taste with salt and pepper. The sauce is now ready to serve.

C H A P T E R   3

Vinaigrettes are used to dress all kinds of salads from tender green leaves to robust, crunchy vegetables. They are also used for hors d'oeuvres — crudités, gourmand salads made with thinly-sliced raw or smoked fish, seafood, baby vegetables, asparagus tips, mange-tout and mushrooms. They even marry well with certain fruits, like citrus, apples and raspberries.

Vinaigrettes,

Flavoured Oils
& Vinegar

Summer is the best time for vinaigrettes, which pep up the appetite, particularly in very hot weather.

Take care never to combine conflicting colours and textures, and do not use too many ingredients which will detract from or spoil the fine flavour of the principal ingredient. By all means be creative, but keep your imagination under control.

Vinaigrettes are all the better for being prepared a few minutes in advance, as they will lose some of their savour and aroma if you make them too long before using them.

The judicious addition of a spoonful of chicken or veal stock, Américaine sauce or a vegetable purée can transform a vinaigrette. Fresh snipped herbs or a touch of spices add the final aesthetic and gustatory note.

A GOOD VINAIGRETTE WILL
ADD LIFE TO ANY SALAD

VINEGARS: *The most commonly-used vinegars are: red wine, white wine, sherry, balsamic, Champagne (which is used for beurre blanc), fruit such as raspberry or blackcurrant (home-made is best), tarragon, cider and garlic-flavoured wine vinegar.*

I have included a recipe for fruit vinegar in this chapter. You do not need one for tarragon vinegar: simply immerse a few sprigs of tarragon in a bottle of white wine vinegar and leave it for several weeks to perfume and flavour the vinegar.

OILS: *The most popular oils are: olive, groundnut, sunflower, corn, rape seed, hazelnut, walnut, sesame, grapeseed and safflower. Some highly-scented oils, like walnut or hazelnut, need to be diluted with a flavourless oil. Use one part flavoured oil to two parts groundnut oil. These oils and vinegars form the basis for every kind of vinaigrette, together with emulsifiers such as cream, yoghurt, fromage blanc, mustard and other refreshing condiments.*

Roquefort Vinaigrette

Vinaigrette au roquefort

I enjoy this dressing in winter served with bitter leaves like dandelion, frisée or escarole. It is also good with crisply-cooked French beans served warm and tossed in the vinaigrette just before serving.

Serves 6
PREPARATION TIME: 5 MINUTES

Ingredients:
3 TBSP WALNUT OIL
3 TBSP SAFFLOWER OR SUNFLOWER OIL
2 TBSP TARRAGON VINEGAR
50G ROQUEFORT, CRUSHED WITH A FORK
1 TSP SNIPPED TARRAGON LEAVES
A FEW DROPS OF WORCESTERSHIRE SAUCE
SALT AND FRESHLY GROUND PEPPER

Combine all the ingredients in a bowl and mix together with a small whisk.

Lavender Vinaigrette

Vinaigrette à la lavande

The flavours of lavender and honey subtly flavour this vinaigrette, which is excellent with raw sliced mushrooms or cucumber, or with tender salad leaves.

Serves 6
PREPARATION TIME: 5 MINUTES

Ingredients:
FLOWERS FROM A STALK OF NOT-TOO-FLOWERY
FRESH LAVENDER
3 TBSP GROUNDNUT OIL
3 TBSP OLIVE OIL
2 TBSP WHITE WINE VINEGAR
1 TSP RUNNY HONEY
LEAVES FROM A SPRIG OF THYME
SALT AND FRESHLY GROUND PEPPER

Put all the ingredients in a blender and whizz for 30 seconds. Season to taste with salt and pepper.

Crustacean Oil Vinaigrette

Vinaigrette à l'huile de crustacés

I serve this vinaigrette at The Waterside Inn with a little dish of freshly-cooked noodles and mixed shellfish — a veritable feast! It is also remarkably good served with poached lobster.

Serves 6
PREPARATION TIME: 5 MINUTES

Ingredients:
100ML CRUSTACEAN OIL (PAGE 47)
1 TBSP WHOLEGRAIN MUSTARD
JUICE OF 1 LEMON
1 TBSP SNIPPED TARRAGON LEAVES
SALT AND FRESHLY GROUND PEPPER

In a bowl, whisk all the ingredients together and season to taste with salt and pepper.

Truffle Vinaigrette

Vinaigrette à la truffe

This vinaigrette is divine with a salad of frisée or escarole, or with baby new potatoes, pasta or tender young leeks, cooked briefly, refreshed and served warm.

Serves 6
PREPARATION TIME: 5 MINUTES

Ingredients:
6 TBSP OLIVE OIL
2 TBSP RED WINE VINEGAR
60G BLACK TRUFFLE, PREFERABLY RAW, FINELY CHOPPED
1/2 SMALL GARLIC CLOVE, VERY FINELY CHOPPED
I ANCHOVY FILLET, RINSED IN COLD WATER AND VERY FINELY CHOPPED
2 HARD-BOILED EGG YOLKS, RUBBED THROUGH A SIEVE OR FINELY CHOPPED
SALT AND FRESHLY GROUND PEPPER

Combine all the ingredients except the egg yolks in a bowl and mix with a spoon. Season with salt and pepper and stir in the egg yolks just before serving.

Basil Vinaigrette

Vinaigrette au basilic

Use this vinaigrette with fresh pasta, green beans and potato salad.

Serves 6
PREPARATION TIME: 5 MINUTES

Ingredients:
6 TBSP OLIVE OIL
2 TBSP RED WINE VINEGAR
15G BASIL LEAVES, SNIPPED
I SMALL GARLIC CLOVE, FINELY CHOPPED
30G SHALLOT, FINELY CHOPPED
40G VERY RIPE TOMATOES
SALT AND FRESHLY GROUND PEPPER

Put all the ingredients in a blender and whizz for 30 seconds. Season to taste with salt and pepper.

Tea Vinaigrette

Vinaigrette au thé

This light, refreshing dressing is perfect for a simple green salad. Choose the variety of tea according to your taste.

Serves 6
PREPARATION TIME: 5 MINUTES
COOKING TIME: ABOUT 2 MINUTES

Ingredients:
3 TBSP WHITE WINE VINEGAR
2 TSP CEYLON TEA LEAVES
120ML SUNFLOWER OIL
I TBSP SNIPPED FLAT PARSLEY LEAVES
SALT AND FRESHLY GROUND PEPPER

In a small saucepan, bring the vinegar to the boil and immediately add the tea. Turn off the heat, cover the pan, leave to cool for 10 minutes, then strain through a wire-mesh conical sieve into a bowl. Mix in the other ingredients with a spoon and season to taste.

Parmesan Vinaigrette

Vinaigrette à la crème
et au parmesan

This dressing goes well with raw chicory, spinach or sliced mushrooms. If it seems too thick, thin it with a little vegetable stock or warm water.

Serves 6
PREPARATION TIME: 5 MINUTES

Ingredients:
I TSP ENGLISH MUSTARD POWDER
2 TBSP CHAMPAGNE VINEGAR
6 TBSP DOUBLE CREAM
30G FRESHLY GRATED PARMESAN
I TBSP SNIPPED CHIVES
SALT AND FRESHLY GROUND PEPPER

In a bowl, stir the mustard powder into the vinegar, then add the other ingredients and season.

Garlic Vinaigrette

Vinaigrette à l'ail

Cooked garlic is delicious and easy to digest. This vinaigrette with its delicate aroma is perfect for well-flavoured mixed salads. Adjust the quantity of garlic to suit your own taste.

Serves 6
PREPARATION TIME: 5 MINUTES
COOKING TIME: ABOUT 10 MINUTES

Ingredients:
A HANDFUL OF COARSE COOKING SALT
6 FINE PLUMP GARLIC CLOVES
2 TBSP BALSAMIC VINEGAR
3 TBSP GROUNDNUT OIL
3 TBSP WALNUT OIL
1 TBSP SNIPPED CHIVES
SALT AND FRESHLY GROUND PEPPER

Preheat the oven to 180°C/350°F/gas mark 4. Spread the coarse salt over a small roasting pan, arrange the garlic cloves on top and bake in the oven for 10 minutes. To check whether the garlic is cooked, insert the tip of a knife into the centre; it should not meet any resistance. Remove the garlic cloves and use a fork to squash them out of their skins, one at a time. Place them on a plate.

Scrape the garlic purée into a bowl, add the vinegar and salt and pepper to taste and whisk until amalgamated, then whisk in the two oils. Just before serving, stir in the chives.

Thai Vinaigrette with Lemon Grass

Vinaigrette thai à la citronnelle

This refreshing vinaigrette is ideal for seasoning crisp salad leaves like cos lettuce or batavia. It makes an excellent dressing for rice noodles which have been infused for 5 minutes in boiling water and refreshed in cold water. The addition of a few prawns, sesame seeds and some extra coriander leaves makes it even more tempting.

Serves 10
PREPARATION TIME: 5 MINUTES, PLUS 2 HOURS'
INFUSING

Ingredients:
2 CM PIECE OF LEMON GRASS, FINELY CHOPPED
15 G CORIANDER LEAVES, FINELY SHREDDED
10 G CHIVES, FINELY SNIPPED
2 TBSP THAI FISH SAUCE
1 TSP SOY SAUCE
200 ML SUNFLOWER OIL
50 ML RICE WINE VINEGAR
FRESHLY GROUND BLACK PEPPER

Mix all the ingredients together in a bowl, season with pepper to taste, cover with cling film and leave the vinaigrette to infuse for 2 hours before using it.

SALAD OF RICE NOODLES AND
PRAWNS, DRESSED WITH THAI
VINAIGRETTE WITH LEMON
GRASS AND CORIANDER SPRIGS

Cucumber Vinaigrette

Vinaigrette de concombre

This sauce is particularly nice in summer, served with green beans cooked al dente, *or thinly-sliced button mushrooms.*

Serves 4
PREPARATION TIME: 10 MINUTES

Special equipment:
A MANDOLINE OR VEGETABLE GRATER

Ingredients:
250G CUCUMBER
60G SHALLOT, FINELY CHOPPED
1 TSP SNIPPED CHIVES
1 TSP SNIPPED TARRAGON
1 TSP SNIPPED FLAT PARSLEY OR CHERVIL
6 TBSP OLIVE OIL
2 TBSP RICE WINE VINEGAR
SALT AND FRESHLY GROUND PEPPER

Peel the cucumber with a potato peeler, halve it lengthways, scoop out the seeds, then slice it as thinly as possible on the mandoline or with the grater. Place in a bowl and add all the other ingredients, seasoning to taste with salt and pepper. Cover with cling film until needed.

Saffron Vinaigrette

Vinaigrette au safran

This vinaigrette is especially delicious served with a mixed salad of tender leaves like lambs' lettuce or oak leaf lettuce garnished with scallops or warm grilled langoustine tails and a few coriander leaves.

Serves 6
PREPARATION TIME: 5 MINUTES

Ingredients:
3 TBSP WHITE WINE VINEGAR
A GENEROUS PINCH OF SAFFRON THREADS
6 TBSP GROUNDNUT OIL
1 TBSP SESAME OIL
1 TSP SOY SAUCE
SALT AND CAYENNE PEPPER

In a small saucepan, warm the vinegar, add the saffron, turn off the heat and infuse until cold. Whisk in all the other ingredients. The vinaigrette is now ready to serve.

Citrus Vinaigrette

Vinaigrette aux agrumes

This vinaigrette is good with all salads, particularly winter salad leaves such as escarole, chicory, frisée and radicchio.

Serves 6
PREPARATION TIME: 5 MINUTES
COOKING TIME: 2 MINUTES

Ingredients:
ZEST OF 1 ORANGE, CUT INTO FINE JULIENNE AND BLANCHED
JUICE OF THE ORANGE
1 TBSP CASTER SUGAR
1 TSP DIJON MUSTARD
ZEST OF 1 LEMON, CUT INTO FINE JULIENNE AND BLANCHED
JUICE OF THE LEMON
6 TBSP GROUNDNUT OIL
1 TBSP FINELY CHOPPED PARSLEY
SALT AND FRESHLY GROUND PEPPER

Put the orange zests and juice and the sugar in a small saucepan and reduce by two-thirds over low heat. Keep at room temperature.

In a bowl, whisk together the mustard, lemon juice and salt and pepper to taste. Whisk in the oil, then the reduced orange juice and zest. Just before serving, stir in the lemon zest and parsley.

Maman Roux's Vinaigrette

Vinaigrette Maman Roux

My mother's creamy vinaigrette has been a favourite of mine since childhood. It is excellent with garden lettuce and escarole.

Ingredients:
1 TBSP FRESHLY GRATED HORSERADISH (BOTTLED
WILL DO AT A PINCH)
JUICE OF 1 LEMON
1 TBSP WHITE WINE TARRAGON VINEGAR
6 TBSP DOUBLE CREAM
40G SHALLOT, FINELY CHOPPED
1 TBSP SNIPPED TARRAGON LEAVES
SALT AND FRESHLY GROUND PEPPER

Whisk together the horseradish, lemon juice, vinegar and seasoning. Gently stir in the cream. If necessary, thin the sauce with $^1/_2$ tbsp warm water. Add the shallot and tarragon just before mixing the dressing into the salad.

Warm Vinaigrette

Vinaigrette tiède

An excellent vinaigrette for substantial mixed salads. Base the dressing on the main ingredient — Américaine sauce for seafood, veal stock for rabbit, chicken livers etc. Or use the deglazing juices from roast chicken or roast meats as a basis for the vinaigrette.

Serves 6
PREPARATION TIME: 5 MINUTES

Ingredients:
2 TBSP VEAL STOCK (PAGE 16)
OR AMÉRICAINE SAUCE (PAGE 90)
5 TBSP OLIVE OIL
3 TBSP SHERRY VINEGAR
1 SPRIG OF FRESH THYME, FINELY CHOPPED
SALT AND FRESHLY GROUND PEPPER

Heat the veal stock or Américaine sauce to 60–80°C, then vigorously whisk in all the other ingredients. Serve the sauce immediately, while it is still tepid.

Anchovy Vinaigrette

Vinaigrette à l'anchois

Serve pan-fried fillets of red mullet, bream or bass, or tender cooked artichokes with a drizzle of this anchovy vinaigrette.

Serves 6
PREPARATION TIME: 5 MINUTES
COOKING TIME: ABOUT 5 MINUTES

Ingredients:
3 TBSP OLIVE OIL
1 GARLIC CLOVE, FINELY CHOPPED
75ML VEGETABLE STOCK (PAGE 22)
3 ANCHOVY FILLETS, FINELY CHOPPED
6 GREEN OLIVES, FINELY CHOPPED
2 TBSP BALSAMIC VINEGAR
SALT AND FRESHLY GROUND PEPPER

In a small saucepan, heat the oil to about 50°C, add the garlic and infuse for 30 seconds. Add the stock and heat to 50–60°C. Turn off the heat, whisk in the other ingredients and season to taste. Serve tepid.

Low Calorie Vinaigrette

Vinaigrette diététique

This flavoursome diet dressing marries well with most salads.

Serves 6
PREPARATION TIME: 5 MINUTES

Ingredients:
1 TSP WHOLEGRAIN MUSTARD
JUICE OF 2 LEMONS
120ML TOMATO JUICE, PREFERABLY FRESH
25G ONION, FINELY CHOPPED
2 TBSP OLIVE OIL
1 TBSP SNIPPED BASIL OR TARRAGON LEAVES
SALT AND FRESHLY GROUND PEPPER

In a bowl, whisk together the mustard and lemon juice, then stir in all the other ingredients except the basil or tarragon; add this just before serving the vinaigrette.

Raspberry Vinegar

Vinaigre de framboise

The exceptionally fine aroma of this home-made vinegar makes the effort involved in preparing it well worth while. It can also be made with blackberries or blackcurrants. Fruit vinegars make delicious dressings for modern gourmand salads made with shellfish, raw vegetables, asparagus, artichokes etc. Best of all, they can be used to deglaze the pan juices of pan-fried or roast red meats and especially game; they add an intense and original depth of flavour to the sauce.

If the fruit is not very sweet, increase the quantity of sugar by 10-15%. The precise amount of vinegar obtained will depend on how much juice the fruit contains (this can vary by up to 30%).

Makes about 1 litre
PREPARATION TIME: 15 MINUTES, PLUS 48 HOURS'
MACERATION
COOKING TIME: 1 HOUR

Ingredients:
1.5KG VERY RIPE RASPBERRIES, BLACKBERRIES OR
BLACKCURRANTS
1.25L WHITE WINE VINEGAR
130G SUGAR LUMPS OR GRANULATED SUGAR
200ML WHITE DENATURED ALCOHOL OR COGNAC

Put half the fruit in a non-metallic bowl, cover with vinegar (1), then cover the bowl with a tea towel or cling film and leave in a cool place for 24 hours. This is the first maceration.

After this time, place a fine-mesh sieve over a bowl and drain the first maceration of fruit (2), pressing very lightly with the back of a ladle to extract as much juice as possible without pushing through any pulp (3). You can use small quantities of the pulp in sauces for game, or simply throw it away. Add the remaining fruit to the extracted juice, then proceed as for the first maceration.

When the second 24 hours have elapsed, drain the fruit into a saucepan in the same way as before. Add the sugar and alcohol (4), and leave until the sugar has dissolved. Stand the pan on a sheet of greaseproof paper in a bain-marie filled with water, set over high heat and bring to the boil. Lower the heat so that the water is just bubbling gently and cook the vinegar for 1 hour, adding more water to the bain-marie if necessary. The temperature of the vinegar should remain at a constant 90°C throughout; it must not boil (hence the need for a bain-marie). While it is cooking, skim the surface as often as necessary.

Transfer the vinegar into a non-metallic bowl and leave in a cool place until cold. Strain it through a muslin-lined conical sieve and a funnel into a bottle and cork it. The vinegar is now ready to use, and will keep for 3 weeks in the fridge.

STRAIN THE VINEGAR THROUGH A
MUSLIN-LINED SIEVE AND A
FUNNEL INTO A BOTTLE

Crustacean Oil

Huile de crustacés

This wonderfully delicate oil is one of my favourites. It makes a superb dressing for fantasy seafood salads or warm asparagus spears.

Makes about 1 litre
PREPARATION TIME: 20 MINUTES, PLUS 3 HOURS' DRYING
STERILIZATION TIME: 35–45 MINUTES

Special equipment:
A 1–1.5L KILNER JAR. IDEALLY, THIS SHOULD BE NEW – IF NOT, IT MUST BE SCRUPULOUSLY CLEAN

Ingredients:
1KG LANGOUSTINES OR CRAYFISH, COOKED IN SALTED WATER
1/2 HEAD OF GARLIC, UNPEELED
1 SPRIG OF THYME
2 BAY LEAVES
1 SMALL BUNCH OF TARRAGON
1TSP WHOLE WHITE PEPPERCORNS
1/2 TSP WHOLE CORIANDER SEEDS
APPROXIMATELY 1L GROUNDNUT OR OLIVE OIL
SALT

Preheat the oven to 120°C/250°F/gas mark 1/2. Remove the eyes of the crustaceans and separate the heads, claws and tails. Keep the tails to use as a garnish for fish or serve in a salad as an hors d'oeuvre. Roughly chop the heads and claws with a chef's knife, put them in a roasting pan and place in the oven to dry for 3 hours. Put the dried heads and claws into the kilner jar with the aromatics, fill up with oil to within 2 cm of the top and seal the lid carefully.

To sterilize the oil, you will need a saucepan at least as tall as the jar. Line the bottom and sides of the pan with foil; this will protect the glass, which might explode if it should knock against the side of the pan. Put in the jar and pour in enough water salted with 300g salt per litre of water to come up to the level of the oil in the jar, but not to submerge it. Bring the water to the boil over high heat and boil for 35–45 minutes, depending on the size of the kilner jar.

After sterilization, leave the jar at room temperature until completely cold, then refrigerate for at least 8 days before using the oil. It will keep for months in the sealed sterile jar if stored in a cool place. Once opened, decant the oil into a bottle; it will keep for several weeks in the fridge.

CRUSTACEAN OIL IS DELICIOUS SERVED WITH WARM ASPARAGUS.

ABOVE: SEPARATE THE TAILS FROM THE HEADS AND CLAWS OF THE CRUSTACEANS

LEFT: PUT THE ROUGHLY-CHOPPED HEADS AND CLAWS IN A ROASTING PAN

PUT THE DRIED HEADS AND CLAWS INTO A CLEAN KILNER JAR WITH THE AROMATICS

FILL THE JAR WITH OIL TO WITHIN 2CM OF THE TOP

STERILIZE THE JAR OF OIL IN A FOIL-LINED PAN OF SALTED WATER FOR 35–45 MINUTES

Chilli Pepper Oil

Huile au parfum de piment

Use this oil to add spiciness and zing to pizzas or vinaigrettes.

Makes 500ml
PREPARATION TIME: 5 MINUTES
COOKING TIME: ABOUT 5 MINUTES

Ingredients:
500ML OLIVE OIL
50G MILD FRESH RED CHILLI, FINELY CHOPPED
1 SPRIG OF THYME
1 BAY LEAF
1 UNPEELED GARLIC CLOVE

In a saucepan, heat the oil to about 80°C. Add all the other ingredients and cover the pan. Immediately turn off the heat and leave the oil to cool. Once cold, pass it through a wire-mesh conical sieve, then pour into a bottle and cork it.

Chive-flavoured Oil

Huile au parfum de ciboulette

Drizzle this oil over grilled fish or add some to a vinaigrette to give a pronounced chive flavour.

Makes 500ml
PREPARATION TIME: 5 MINUTES
COOKING TIME: ABOUT 5 MINUTES

Ingredients:
500ML OLIVE OIL
50G CHIVES, SNIPPED

In a saucepan, heat the oil to about 80°C, add the chives and cover the pan. Immediately, turn off the heat and leave the oil to cool. Once cold, whizz in a blender for 30 seconds, then pass the oil through a wire-mesh conical sieve, pour into a bottle and cork it. It will keep for several days.

Bois Boudran Sauce

Sauce Bois Boudran

An excellent sauce for roast chicken or poussin, Bois Boudran sauce can also be used to coat a salmon or lightly poached trout just before serving. I have loved this sauce ever since the days when I cooked for the Rothschild family.

Serves 6
PREPARATION TIME: 5 MINUTES

Ingredients:
150ML GROUNDNUT OIL
50ML WINE VINEGAR
85G TOMATO KETCHUP
1 TSP WORCESTERSHIRE SAUCE
5 DROPS OF TABASCO
100G SHALLOTS, CHOPPED
5G CHERVIL, FINELY SNIPPED
5G CHIVES, FINELY SNIPPED
20G TARRAGON, FINELY SNIPPED
SALT AND FRESHLY GROUND PEPPER

Combine the oil, vinegar, a pinch of salt and three turns of the pepper mill in a bowl. Stir with a small whisk, then add the ketchup, Worcestershire sauce, Tabasco, chopped shallots and all the snipped herbs. Adjust the seasoning with salt and pepper and keep at room temperature; the sauce is ready to use right away, but it can also be kept in an airtight container in the fridge for 3 days.

POACHED SALMON
WITH BOIS BOUDRAN
SAUCE

Pistou Sauce

Sauce au pistou

Pistou smells as good as it tastes. Use it to perfume Mediterranean soups and steamed fish. Its powerful, intoxicating flavour also goes well with pasta.

Serves 6
PREPARATION TIME: 10 MINUTES

Ingredients:
4 GARLIC CLOVES, PEELED, HALVED
AND GREEN SHOOT REMOVED
20 BASIL LEAVES
100G FRESHLY GRATED PARMESAN
150ML OLIVE OIL
SALT AND FRESHLY GROUND PEPPER

In a small mortar, crush the garlic to a purée (1) with a pinch of salt (or use a blender). Add the basil and crush or blend to a homogeneous paste (2). Add the Parmesan (3), then trickle in the olive oil in a steady stream, stirring continuously with the pestle, as though you were making mayonnaise (4). Work the sauce until smooth (5). Season to taste with salt and pepper.

Use the pistou immediately, or transfer it to a bowl and cover with cling film. It will keep in the fridge for several days.

PESTO: If you add 30g grilled or toasted pine kernels together with the basil, you will obtain Italian pesto, which has a firmer, richer consistency. Pesto is perfect stirred into a risotto just before serving, and has many other uses.

PISTOU IS DELICIOUS STIRRED INTO
VEGETABLE SOUPS

❶ ❷ ❸ ❹

Piquant Fromage Blanc Sauce

Sauce piquant au fromage blanc

This sauce is most agreeable served with a cold vegetable terrine or a warm pizza-style tomato and courgette tart.

Serves 8
PREPARATION TIME: 5 MINUTES

Ingredients:
400G FROMAGE BLANC, WHICHEVER FAT CONTENT
YOU PREFER
SEEDS FROM 2 PASSION FRUIT, SCOOPED OUT WITH A
SPOON
4 TBSP RASPBERRY VINEGAR,
HOME-MADE (PAGE 44) OR SHOP-BOUGHT
1 TBSP FINELY SNIPPED LEMON VERBENA
1/2 TBSP SOFT GREEN PEPPERCORNS, WELL DRAINED
AND CHOPPED
SALT AND CAYENNE PEPPER

Put all the ingredients in a bowl and mix together with a spoon. Season with salt and plenty of cayenne.

Avocado Sauce

Sauce à l'avocat

Serve this sauce as a dip for raw vegetables, such as carrots, cauliflower, cucumber or radishes, or with cold langoustines or cooked mussels.

Serves 6
PREPARATION TIME: 5 MINUTES

Ingredients:
1 AVOCADO, ABOUT 300G, PEELED AND STONED
300G PLAIN YOGHURT
2 TBSP DILL, SNIPPED
2 TBSP LEMON JUICE
1 TSP STRONG DIJON MUSTARD
A SMALL PINCH OF CURRY POWDER
SALT AND FRESHLY GROUND PEPPER

Combine all the ingredients in a blender and whizz for 30 seconds. Adjust the seasoning with salt and pepper.

Ravigote Sauce

Sauce ravigote

This sauce gives an extra lift to offal such as lamb's or calf's brains, tongue, feet, head etc. I also like to serve it with potatoes boiled in their skins; leave your guests to peel their own potatoes and dip them in the sauce as they eat.

Serves 6
PREPARATION TIME: 5 MINUTES

Ingredients:
6 TBSP GROUNDNUT OR SUNFLOWER OIL
2 TBSP WHITE WINE VINEGAR
1 TBSP SMALL CAPERS (CHOP THEM IF THEY
ARE LARGE)
1 TBSP CORNICHONS OR SMALL GHERKINS,
FINELY DICED
4 TBSP FINES HERBES (PAGE 10), FINELY SNIPPED
30G ONION, FINELY CHOPPED
SALT AND FRESHLY GROUND PEPPER

Combine all the ingredients in a bowl and mix thoroughly.

Oregano and Sun-dried Tomato Sauce with Basil Oil

Sauce à l'origan et aux tomates séchées, à l'huile de basilic

This sun-dried tomato sauce makes an excellent accompaniment to grilled veal chops and tournedos, or robust grilled fish like tuna or monkfish.

Serves 8
PREPARATION TIME: 10 MINUTES

Ingredients:
160G SUN-DRIED TOMATOES IN OLIVE OIL
180G VERY RIPE FRESH TOMATOES
200ML CHICKEN STOCK (PAGE 18)
40ML BALSAMIC VINEGAR
1 TBSP FRESH OREGANO LEAVES, FINELY CHOPPED
SALT AND FRESHLY GROUND PEPPER

For the basil oil:
60ML EXTRA VIRGIN OLIVE OIL
10G FRESH BASIL LEAVES

Combine the sun-dried and fresh tomatoes, chicken stock and balsamic vinegar in the bowl of a food processor. Whizz for 2 minutes, then strain the sauce through a conical sieve into a bowl. Add the chopped oregano and season with salt and pepper.

To make the basil oil, put the oil and basil in the clean bowl of the food processor. Season to taste with salt and pepper and whizz for 2 minutes. Pour the oil straight into a bowl (do not strain it).

Serve the tomato sauce either tepid or cold, poured in a ribbon around the meat or fish, then sprinkled with a few drops of basil oil.

Sauce Vierge

I serve this sauce with lobster cappelletti, steamed fillets of red mullet and sea bass and fresh pasta.

Serves 6
PREPARATION TIME: 5 MINUTES

Ingredients:
200ML OLIVE OIL
80G TOMATOES, PEELED, DESEEDED AND
FINELY DICED
JUICE OF 1 LEMON
2 TBSP SNIPPED BASIL LEAVES
1 TBSP SNIPPED CHERVIL LEAVES
1 GARLIC CLOVE, FINELY CHOPPED
6 CORIANDER SEEDS, CRUSHED
SALT AND FRESHLY GROUND PEPPER

Combine the ingredients in a bowl, mix gently and season. Just before serving, warm the sauce to about 30–40°C.

Flavoured butters are tasty, simple to prepare and come in a range of attractive colours, from pastel to vibrant, depending on their composition. They can be used instead of a sauce (allow 30g per person) and as a topping for vegetables or poached, pan-fried or grilled fish and meat.

F lavoured Butters

& Vegetable Coulis

I usually roll the butters into a sausage shape, using cling film, but if you prefer, they can be piped into rosettes using a piping bag with a fluted nozzle. Many make delicious canapés; soften the butter slightly and spread or pipe it on to toasted croûtons.

The butters are at their most flavoursome made just before serving and firmed up for a few minutes in the fridge, but they can be kept refrigerated for three or four days, or frozen for several weeks. That way, you can always add extra flavour to a dish in a matter of moments.

I use my flavoured butters to enhance a sauce, to refine it (with foie gras butter, for example) or to personalize it as the mood takes me with the flavour of vegetables, herbs or shellfish. This chapter contains my particular favourites, but you can create dozens of other butters, using mustard, olives, truffles, tomato ... let your imagination run riot.

Vegetable coulis are also extremely useful and taste wonderful. These are champion sauces, light, insubstantial and quick to prepare. Some contain cream, but this can be replaced by fromage blanc if you prefer. Do not cook this in the sauce, but add it at the last moment and give it just a brief bubble. These coulis should be served in a sauceboat, or spread thinly over a plate and topped with the accompanying fish or meat.

Vegetable Butter

Beurre de légumes

This butter is ideal as a liaison for a béchamel sauce (page 128) or chicken velouté (page 132), lifting them out of the ordinary with its special flavour and perfect colour. A few discs make a most delicious topping for boiled potatoes.

Makes about 260g
PREPARATION TIME: 10 MINUTES

Ingredients:
150G VEGETABLES OF YOUR CHOICE, EG CARROTS,
FRENCH BEANS OR ASPARAGUS
150G BUTTER, SOFTENED

Peel or trim and wash the vegetables and cook them in lightly salted water until tender. Refresh, drain and pat dry with a cloth.

Put the cooked vegetables and the butter in a food processor and whizz for about 3 minutes, scraping the ingredients into the centre of the bowl every minute to make a homogeneous mixture. If you don't have a food processor, use a pestle and mortar.

Using a plastic scraper, rub the flavoured butter through a drum sieve to eliminate any vegetable fibres. Using cling film, roll it into one or two sausage shapes and refrigerate or freeze until ready to use.

Maître d'Hôtel Butter

Beurre maître d'hôtel

This classic topping remains a favourite for grilled meat or fish.

Makes about 175g
PREPARATION TIME: 5 MINUTES

Ingredients:
150G BUTTER, SOFTENED
20G PARSLEY, CHOPPED
JUICE OF $1/2$ LEMON
SALT
A PINCH OF CAYENNE PEPPER OR FRESHLY GROUND
BLACK PEPPER

Using a wooden spoon, work the parsley into the butter, then mix in the lemon juice. Season to taste and, using cling film, roll the butter into one or two sausage shapes. Refrigerate or freeze until needed.

Horseradish Butter

Beurre de raifort

Finish a sauce Albert (page 132) with this delicious butter, or use it to pep up a béchamel (page 128). It also goes well with any grilled white meat.

Makes about 200g
PREPARATION TIME: 7 MINUTES

Ingredients:
50G FRESHLY GRATED HORSERADISH
150G BUTTER, SOFTENED
SALT AND FRESHLY GROUND PEPPER

Pulverize the horseradish with a pestle in a mortar, adding the butter a little at a time. When it is all well mixed, use a plastic scraper to rub the seasoned butter through a drum sieve and season to taste with salt and pepper. Using cling film, roll it into one or two sausage shapes and refrigerate or freeze until needed.

Langoustine Butter

Beurre de langoustines

Enrich fish sauces with this butter. It makes wonderful canapés spread on toast croûtons and topped with langoustine tails.

Makes about 500g
PREPARATION TIME: 15 MINUTES
COOKING TIME: ABOUT 20 MINUTES

Ingredients:
50G BUTTER, PREFERABLY CLARIFIED (PAGE 31)
1 SMALL CARROT, FINELY DICED
1 MEDIUM ONION, FINELY DICED
12 CRAYFISH OR LANGOUSTINES, LIVE IF POSSIBLE
5 TBSP COGNAC OR ARMAGNAC
200ML WHITE WINE
1 SMALL BOUQUET GARNI (PAGE 10)
2 PINCHES OF CAYENNE PEPPER
SOFTENED BUTTER, 75% OF THE WEIGHT OF THE
COOKED CRUSTACEAN HEADS AND CLAWS
SALT AND FRESHLY GROUND PEPPER

Melt the clarified butter in a deep frying pan, add the diced carrot and onion and sweat until soft. Using a slotted spoon, transfer the vegetables to a ramekin, leaving the cooking butter in the pan.

Put the crustaceans in the pan and sauté over high heat for 2 minutes. Add the Cognac, ignite it, then moisten with the white wine. Add the cooked diced vegetables, bouquet garni, a little cayenne and a small pinch of salt and cook gently over low heat for 10 minutes. Tip all the contents of the pan into a bowl and leave to cool completely at room temperature.

To make the flavoured butter, separate the crayfish or langoustine heads and tails. Keep the tails for another use (as an hors d'oeuvre salad or canapés, for example). Gather up the heads and claws, and the creamy flesh from the heads and weigh them. Put them in a food processor or blender with 75% of their weight of softened butter and the diced vegetables, and whizz until mushy. Using a plastic scraper, rub through a drum sieve and season to taste. Using cling film, roll the flavoured butter into one or two sausage shapes and refrigerate or freeze until needed.

Pistachio Butter

Beurre de pistaches

I use this butter in my Sauternes sauce with pistachios (page 102) or add it to a hollandaise (page 116) to give a touch of mellowness.

Makes about 250g
PREPARATION TIME: 7 MINUTES

Ingredients:
100G RAW SKINNED PISTACHIO NUTS
150G BUTTER, SOFTENED
SALT AND FRESHLY GROUND PEPPER

Pound the pistachios to a paste with 1 tbsp water in a mortar or food processor. Add all the butter at once, mix and season, then rub through a drum sieve with a plastic scraper. Using cling film, roll the pistachio butter into one or two sausage shapes and refrigerate or freeze until ready to use.

Anchovy Butter

Beurre d'anchois

Use this delicious butter on grilled fish, or serve it on toast canapés topped with a julienne of anchovy fillets.

Makes about 180g
PREPARATION TIME: 7 MINUTES

Ingredients:
50G ANCHOVY FILLETS IN OIL
150G BUTTER, SOFTENED
SALT AND FRESHLY GROUND PEPPER

Chop the anchovy fillets or pound them in a mortar. Using a wooden spoon, mix them into the butter and, using a plastic scraper, rub through a drum sieve or whizz in a food processor. Season, being circumspect with the salt, as the anchovies already contain plenty. Use cling film to roll the butter into one or two sausage shapes and refrigerate or freeze until ready to use.

POUND TO A PASTE

RUB THE PASTE THROUGH
A DRUM SIEVE

THE BUTTER SHOULD
NOT CONTAIN ANY HARD
GRAINS OF CHEESE

Goat's Cheese Butter

Beurre de fromage de chèvre

Discs of goat's cheese butter make an appetizing topping for grilled white meats, like veal escalopes or chicken wings. The butter is also delicious with pasta; mix it in just before serving and add a little snipped basil or flat-leaf parsley to enhance the flavour of the cheesy butter.

Makes about 300g
PREPARATION TIME: 5 MINUTES

Ingredients:
150G FRESH OR SEMI-HARD GOAT'S CHEESE,
WHICHEVER YOU PREFER
150G BUTTER, SOFTENED

Cut up the goat's cheese, put it in a mortar or food processor with the butter and pound with a pestle or process for about 3 minutes, scraping the butter and cheese towards the centre of the bowl every minute to obtain a completely homogeneous mixture. Using a plastic scraper rub the flavoured butter through a drum sieve to eliminate any hard grains of cheese, then, using cling film, roll it into one or two sausage shapes. Refrigerate or freeze until ready to use.

RIGHT: COMBINE THE CHEESE
AND BUTTER IN A MORTAR

PUT THE BUTTER ON TO A
SHEET OF CLING FILM

ROLL THE BUTTER INTO A
SAUSAGE SHAPE IN THE
CLING FILM

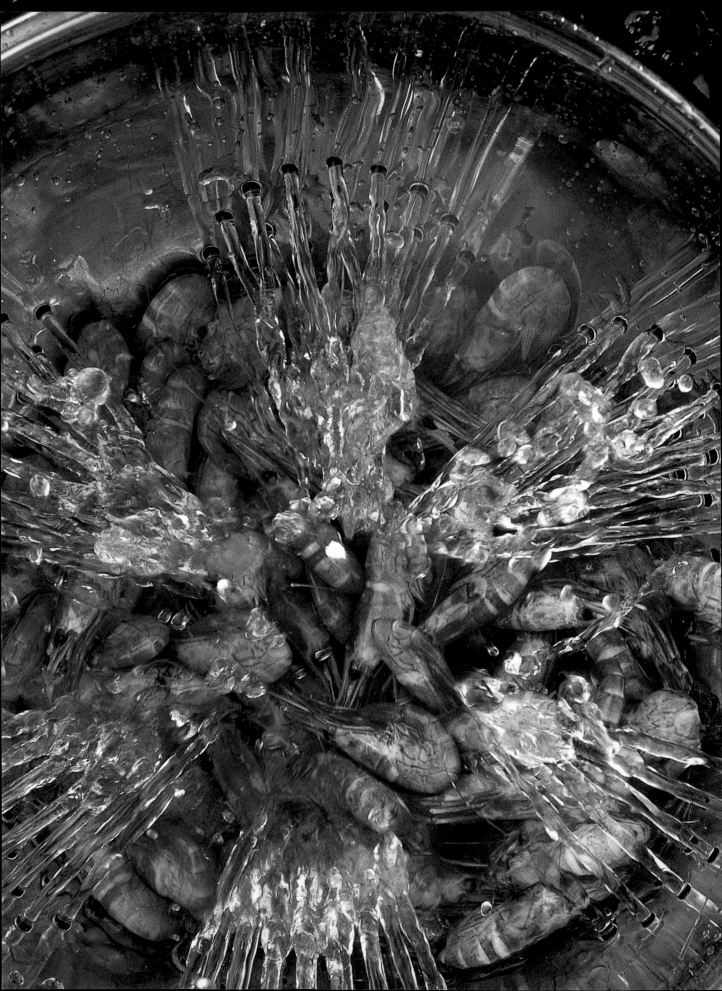

Shrimp Butter

Beurre de crevettes

LEFT: WASH THE SHRIMPS IN
COLD WATER

*Discs of shrimp butter add a special something to pan-fried or
grilled fish. It can be used to enrich a fish sauce, or served as
canapés spread on toasted croûtons. For extra zing, add a pinch
of cayenne pepper.*

Makes about 220g
PREPARATION TIME: 10 MINUTES

Ingredients:
150G VERY FRESH PINK OR BROWN SHRIMPS
150G BUTTER, SOFTENED
CAYENNE PEPPER (OPTIONAL)

Rinse the shrimps in cold water, leaving any eggs
attached, drain and pat dry in a tea towel.

Place the shrimps in a blender with the butter and a
pinch of cayenne, if you like. Process for about 3
minutes, scraping the ingredients into the centre of the
bowl every minute, to obtain a homogeneous mixture.
If you prefer, you can use a pestle and mortar instead of
a blender.

Using a plastic scraper, rub the flavoured butter
through a drum sieve to eliminate the shrimp shells.
Using cling film, roll it into one or two sausage shapes
and refrigerate or freeze until ready to use.

PROCESS WITH BUTTER
TO A PASTE

RUB THE SHRIMP BUTTER
THROUGH A SIEVE

PUT THE SHRIMPS IN A
BLENDER

PAN-FRIED FISH TOPPED WITH SHRIMP
BUTTER

Roquefort Butter

Beurre de roquefort

Use this butter as a delicious spread for toast canapés, or whisk it into a fish velouté to add extra character and piquancy. This is particularly good with cooked shelled mussels served in ramekins. A tablespoon of roquefort butter added to a sauce for poultry is also surprisingly good.

Makes 250g
PREPARATION TIME: 5 MINUTES

Ingredients:
150G BUTTER, SOFTENED
100G ROQUEFORT
FRESHLY GROUND PEPPER

Crumble the roquefort and work it into the softened butter with a wooden spoon. Using a plastic scraper, rub it through a drum sieve and season with pepper. Using cling film, roll the butter into one or two sausage shapes and refrigerate or freeze until ready to use.

Barbecue Butter

Beurre barbecue

This butter enhances the flavour of any barbecued meats. Brush it over the cooked meat just before serving.

Makes about 175g
PREPARATION TIME: 7 MINUTES

Ingredients:
150G BUTTER, SOFTENED
1 TBSP CHILLI SAUCE
1 TBSP RUNNY HONEY
1 TBSP LEMON JUICE
10G MINT LEAVES, SHREDDED
SALT AND FRESHLY GROUND PEPPER

Using a wooden spoon, mix the ingredients one a time into the softened butter, adding the mint last of all. Season to taste. The butter is ready to use immediately. Keep it at room temperature.

Caviar Butter

Beurre de caviar

Serve this flavoursome, delicate butter in a sauceboat to accompany grilled fillets of sole or John Dory. It is best to use it on the day it is made, without refrigerating or freezing it.

Makes about 200g
PREPARATION TIME: 5 MINUTES

Ingredients:
60G CAVIAR, PREFERABLY PRESSED (OTHERWISE USE SEVRUGA)
150G BUTTER, SOFTENED
SALT AND FRESHLY GROUND PEPPER

Using a wooden spoon, mix the caviar into the butter, then, using a plastic scraper, rub it through a drum sieve. Season to taste and use on the same day.

Crab Butter

Beurre de tourteau

Serve crab butter on toast canapés, or use it to add extra body to sauces for scallops and seafood.

Makes about 300g
PREPARATION TIME: 7 MINUTES

Ingredients:
150G OF THE YELLOWISH-GREY MEAT FROM INSIDE A CRAB SHELL
150G BUTTER, SOFTENED
1 TBSP COGNAC
1 TSP HARISSA, OR 5 DROPS OF TABASCO
JUICE OF 1/2 LEMON
SALT AND FRESHLY GROUND PEPPER

Whizz the crab meat and butter in a blender for 3 minutes. Rub through a drum sieve then, with a wooden spoon, mix in the Cognac, harissa or Tabasco and the lemon juice and season. Using cling film, roll the butter into one or two sausage shapes and refrigerate or freeze until needed.

Paprika Butter

Beurre de paprika

This butter is perfect served with grilled escalopes of veal, turkey or chicken.

Makes about 180g
PREPARATION TIME: 10 MINUTES

Ingredients:
20G BUTTER
30G ONION, FINELY CHOPPED
150G BUTTER, SOFTENED
1/2-1 TBSP PAPRIKA, ACCORDING TO TASTE
SALT AND FRESHLY GROUND PEPPER

Melt the 20g butter in a small saucepan, add the onion and sweat gently for 2 minutes. Leave to cool and, as soon as the onion is completely cold, mix it into the softened butter with a wooden spoon. Add the paprika and season to taste with salt and pepper. Using a plastic scraper, rub the flavoured butter through a sieve or whizz in a food processor. Using cling film, roll it into one or two sausage shapes and refrigerate or freeze until needed.

CURRY BUTTER: This can be made in the same way; just double the quantity of onion and the butter to sweat it in, and replace the paprika with 1-2 tablespoons curry powder, according to taste. Add the curry to the onions after 1 minute, not directly to the softened butter. Curry butter can be used with the same meats as paprika butter, and also with grilled pork chops.

Foie Gras Butter

Beurre de foie gras

This creamy, delicate and tasty butter is excellent on toast canapés. A few discs add a wonderful flavour to a grilled steak, but best of all, it gives a superb velvety, unctuous finish to many sauces, such as allemande (page 139), Périgueux (page 144) and port (page 74).

Makes about 200g
PREPARATION TIME: 5 MINUTES

Ingredients:
100G BUTTER, SOFTENED
100G TERRINE OR BALLOTINE OF DUCK OR GOOSE
FOIE GRAS
2 TBSP ARMAGNAC OR COGNAC
SALT AND FRESHLY GROUND PEPPER

Mix all the ingredients with a wooden spoon, seasoning to taste with salt and pepper. Using a plastic scraper, rub through a drum sieve or whizz in a blender. Using cling film, roll the butter into one or two sausage shapes and refrigerate or freeze until needed.

Red Pepper Butter

Beurre de poivron rouge

Like anchovy butter, red pepper butter is excellent spread on toast canapés, and accompanies poached fish extremely well. Whisked into sauces, such as hollandaise (page 116), béchamel (page 128) or devil sauce (page 152), this butter will enhance the flavour and colour and add a touch of originality.

Makes about 200g
PREPARATION TIME: 10 MINUTES

Ingredients:
20G BUTTER
60G RED PEPPER, FINELY DICED
I SPRIG OF THYME
150G BUTTER, SOFTENED
SALT AND FRESHLY GROUND BLACK PEPPER

Melt the 20g butter in a small saucepan and add the diced pepper and thyme. Sweat gently for 5 minutes, then leave at room temperature until cold. Mix the cooked red pepper into the butter with a wooden spoon, then use a plastic scraper to rub the butter through a drum sieve or whizz in a blender. Using cling film, roll the butter into one or two sausage shapes and refrigerate or freeze until ready to use.

Asparagus Coulis

Coulis d'asperges

This delicious sauce is almost as light as a nage. I add some asparagus tips at the last moment and serve it with delicate steamed fish, or pour it around my vegetable lasagne to make a dish which even non-vegetarians love.

Serves 8
PREPARATION TIME: 10 MINUTES
COOKING TIME: ABOUT 40 MINUTES

Ingredients:
350G ASPARAGUS SPEARS, PREFERABLY SMALL ONES
50G BUTTER
80G SHALLOTS, CHOPPED
I SPRIG OF THYME
300ML CHICKEN STOCK (PAGE 18), OR WATER
500ML DOUBLE CREAM
I TSP SOY SAUCE (OPTIONAL)
SALT AND FRESHLY GROUND PEPPER

Peel the asparagus stalks with a vegetable peeler. Cut off the tips and blanch them in boiling salted water. Refresh, drain and set aside. Chop the stalks and leave them raw.

In a thick-bottomed saucepan, melt the butter, add the chopped asparagus stalks and shallot and sweat gently for 5 minutes. Add the thyme and chicken stock or water and cook over medium heat for 15 minutes. Pour in the cream, increase the heat to high and reduce the coulis by one-third. Whizz in a blender for 3 minutes, then pass through a conical sieve. Season with salt and pepper to taste, adding the soy sauce if you wish. Keep the coulis warm until needed.

Chilled Vegetable Coulis

Coulis de légumes glacés

These chilled vegetable coulis make excellent accompaniments to cold poached fish served as part of a buffet, or by themselves as a summer hors d'oeuvre. I sometimes serve three different coulis (carrot, celeriac and peas) as an attractive, mellow amuse-gueule, placing a tablespoon of each on a small plate, to be eaten with a teaspoon.

Serves 6
PREPARATION TIME: 10 MINUTES
COOKING TIME: 5–20 MINUTES, DEPENDING ON THE VEGETABLES

Ingredients:
360G CARROTS OR CELERIAC, PEELED AND DICED, OR 360G FRENCH BEANS, OR 500G SHELLED FRESH PEAS
500ML DOUBLE CREAM
SALT AND FRESHLY GROUND PEPPER

Cook your chosen vegetable in boiling salted water until tender. Drain and whizz in a blender with 100ml cream to make a very smooth purée. Transfer to a bowl and leave to cool, stirring from time to time. Using a whisk, gently stir in the rest of the cream. Season the coulis to taste with salt and pepper and chill in the fridge until needed.

Raw Tomato Coulis

Coulis de tomates crues

I adore this coulis served with cold poached eggs or as a sauce for cold pasta – a simple, refreshing summer dish which is very quick to prepare.

Serves 6
PREPARATION TIME: 5 MINUTES

Ingredients:
350G VERY RIPE TOMATOES, PURÉED THEN RUBBED THROUGH A SIEVE TO GIVE ABOUT 250ML JUICE AND PULP
60ML SHERRY VINEGAR (PREFERABLY), OR BALSAMIC VINEGAR
8 CORIANDER SEEDS, CRUSHED
12 BASIL LEAVES, SHREDDED
1 TSP TOMATO CONCENTRATE (OPTIONAL)
100ML OLIVE OIL
SALT AND FRESHLY GROUND PEPPER

Put all the ingredients in a bowl, except the basil leaves. Mix with a whisk, season with salt and pepper, then add the basil. The coulis is ready to serve. Alternatively, transfer it to an airtight container and refrigerate; it will keep well for 3 days.

Cooked Tomato Coulis

Coulis de tomates cuites

This tomato coulis is extremely versatile, and I use it frequently in my kitchen. It is divine spread over a plate and topped with grilled fish. Alternatively add a small quantity to a fish sauce, or, better still, a béchamel (page 128) for a gratin of fresh pasta.

Serves 4
PREPARATION TIME: 5 MINUTES
COOKING TIME: ABOUT 1 HOUR

Ingredients:
150ML OLIVE OIL
2 GARLIC CLOVES, CRUSHED
60G SHALLOTS, FINELY CHOPPED
1 SMALL BOUQUET GARNI (PAGE 10),
CONTAINING PLENTY OF THYME
750G VERY RIPE MARMANDE TOMATOES,
PEELED, DESEEDED AND CHOPPED
1 TBSP TOMATO CONCENTRATE (ONLY IF THE
TOMATOES ARE NOT RIPE ENOUGH)
A PINCH OF SUGAR
6 PEPPERCORNS, CRUSHED
SALT

In a thick-bottomed saucepan, warm the olive oil with the garlic, shallot and bouquet garni. After 2 minutes, add the tomatoes, tomato purée if needed, sugar and crushed peppercorns, and cook very gently for about 1 hour, stirring occasionally with a wooden spoon until all the moisture has evaporated. Remove the bouquet garni and whizz the contents of the pan in a blender to make a smooth purée. Season to taste. The coulis is ready to use immediately, but you can keep it in an airtight container in the fridge for 5 days.

If the sauce is to be served plain, after reheating, add a little olive oil just before serving.

HOW TO PEEL TOMATOES: Cut a cross in the top of the tomatoes and gouge out the cores. Drop the tomatoes into boiling water until the skin starts to split (about 10–20 seconds) then take them out (1) and plunge them into iced water (2). Lift out the tomatoes with a draining spoon (3) and slip off the skins (4).

ADD THE CHOPPED
TOMATOES TO THE
SOFTENED SHALLOTS

COOK THE TOMATOES
UNTIL ALL THE MOISTURE
HAS EVAPORATED

PUT THE CONTENTS OF THE PAN,
EXCEPT THE BOUQUET GARNI, INTO
A BLENDER AND WHIZZ INTO A
SMOOTH PASTE

1 **2**

3 **4**

Light Carrot Coulis

Coulis léger de carottes

This coulis is almost like a jus and should be eaten with a spoon. It goes well with pan-fried scallops and grilled poultry breasts, and also with rice pilaff. I serve it with carrot tart, which is much appreciated by my vegetarian customers. For them, I omit the veal stock and thicken the sauce with a little beurre manié (page 31).

Serves 6
PREPARATION TIME: 5 MINUTES
COOKING TIME: ABOUT 10 MINUTES

Ingredients:
3 CARROTS, TOTAL WEIGHT ABOUT 250G
JUICE OF 2 ORANGES
200ML VEAL STOCK (PAGE 16)
1 TSP FRESHLY GRATED GINGER
60G BUTTER, CHILLED AND DICED
SALT AND FRESHLY GROUND PEPPER

Peel the carrots, cut them into small pieces, then whizz them in a food processor with the orange juice and veal stock for 3 minutes. Transfer to a saucepan, set over high heat and reduce the coulis for about 10 minutes, until it lightly coats the back of a spoon. Add the ginger, take the pan off the heat, and whisk in the butter, a little at a time. Season the coulis to taste, pass it through a conical sieve and serve immediately.

Chicory and Champagne Coulis

Coulis d'endives au Champagne

I love this light, delicate sauce served with poached poussin, chicken or capon, or poured over cauliflower florets in shallow ramekins. The cauliflower must be very tender and not at all crunchy. In season, I put a little truffle in the sauce, which adds a stunning extra dimension — definitely worth trying!

Serves 4
PREPARATION TIME: 20 MINUTES
COOKING TIME: ABOUT 30 MINUTES

Ingredients:
2 HEADS OF CHICORY, TOTAL WEIGHT ABOUT 200G
60G BUTTON MUSHROOMS
50G BUTTER
JUICE OF 1/2 LEMON
A PINCH OF CASTER SUGAR
300ML CHAMPAGNE OR SPARKLING WHITE WINE
200ML DOUBLE CREAM
1 TBSP TRUFFLE JUICE, OR 30G TRUFFLES, FINELY CHOPPED (OPTIONAL)
SALT AND FRESHLY GROUND PEPPER

Slice the chicory and mushrooms very thinly. Melt the butter in a deep frying pan, add the chicory, mushrooms and lemon juice and cook over low heat for 5 minutes, stirring every minute. Add a pinch of sugar, cook for another 2 minutes, then pour in the Champagne, let it bubble for a moment, and finally add the cream. Cook over medium heat until the coulis has reduced by half, purée in a blender for 5 minutes, then pass through a conical sieve. Season with salt and pepper and add the truffle if you wish. Keep the coulis warm and serve it within 10 minutes of blending.

Leek Coulis with Curry

Coulis de poireaux au curry

Spread a spoonful of this coulis over individual plates and top with grilled or pan-fried firm-fleshed fish such as monkfish or turbot, or some langoustines à la meunière.

Serves 8
PREPARATION TIME: 10 MINUTES
COOKING TIME: ABOUT 40 MINUTES

Ingredients:
500G TENDER SMALL OR MEDIUM LEEKS
40G BUTTER
1/2TSP CURRY POWDER
250ML CHICKEN STOCK (PAGE 18)
300ML DOUBLE CREAM
1/2TSP MUSTARD POWDER
SALT AND FRESHLY GROUND PEPPER

Cut off the greenest parts of the leeks and the root ends. Split the leeks lengthways, wash meticulously in cold water, then slice them finely. Blanch in boiling, salted water, refresh and drain.

In a thick-bottomed saucepan, melt the butter and sweat the leeks gently for 10 minutes. Add the curry powder, then the chicken stock and cook over medium heat for 10 minutes. Add the cream and mustard powder and simmer for a further 10 minutes, then whizz in a blender for 5 minutes. Pass the coulis through a conical sieve back into the pan. Season and keep the coulis warm, without letting it boil, until ready to serve.

Morel Coulis

Coulis de morilles

Truly one for mushroom lovers, this coulis is excellent served with pan-fried medallions of veal or fresh pasta; make a well in the middle of the pasta and pour in the coulis. You can substitute button mushrooms for the morels, but of course the flavour will not be as fine.

Serves 8
PREPARATION TIME: 10 MINUTES
COOKING TIME: ABOUT 25 MINUTES

Ingredients:
40G BUTTER
40G SHALLOT, CHOPPED
250G FRESH MORELS, FINELY SLICED, OR 75G DRIED
MORELS, INFUSED IN BOILING WATER FOR
10 MINUTES, THEN FINELY SLICED
300ML CHICKEN STOCK (PAGE 18)
350ML DOUBLE CREAM
60G COOKED OR TINNED DUCK OR GOOSE FOIE GRAS
SALT AND FRESHLY GROUND PEPPER

Melt the butter in a thick-bottomed saucepan. Add the shallot, then the morels and sweat gently for 5 minutes. Add the chicken stock and cook over medium heat for 5 minutes. Next add the cream and, still over medium heat, reduce the coulis by one-third, stirring occasionally with a wooden spoon. Transfer to a blender and process for 5 minutes.

Pass the coulis through a conical sieve back into the saucepan, set over low heat and whisk in the foie gras, a small piece at a time. Season the coulis with salt and pepper and serve immediately or, if necessary, keep it warm on a very low heat for a few minutes.

Parsley Coulis

Coulis de persil

This coulis is delicious served in little ramekins or egg coddlers, topped with a few snails sautéed in noisette butter. When serving the coulis with a grilled veal escalope, I sometimes substitute a pinch of curry powder for the pepper.

Serves 8
PREPARATION TIME: 10 MINUTES
COOKING TIME: 8–10 MINUTES

Ingredients:
400G CURLY OR FLAT-LEAF PARSLEY, STALKS
REMOVED
300ML DOUBLE CREAM
50G SHALLOTS, THINLY SLICED
100ML MILK, AT BOILING POINT
SALT AND FRESHLY GROUND PEPPER

Wash the parsley in plenty of cold water (1). Bring a pan of lightly salted water to the boil and plunge in the parsley (2). Boil for 2 minutes, then refresh in iced water (3), drain, put the parsley in a cloth (4) and squeeze the parsley to eliminate all the water (5).

In a saucepan, boil the cream with the shallots and reduce by one-third. Add the parsley (6) and bubble for 2 minutes, stirring continuously with a wooden spoon. Take the pan off the heat, add the boiling milk and stir. Purée in a blender for 2–3 minutes, until very smooth, then rub through a drum sieve (7), using a plastic scraper. Season with salt and pepper and serve hot, but do not boil the coulis once it has been sieved.

PARSLEY COULIS
TOPPED WITH SNAILS
SAUTÉED IN NOISETTE
BUTTER

All terrines and pâtés — pork, veal, poultry or game — are improved and enhanced by the addition of a sauce or chutney, which is often fruity and refreshing, with a hint of acidity. Such sauces help to develop the flavour of the meats.

Sauces & Chutneys for Terrines, Pâtés & Game

My own favourite is Cumberland sauce; we often serve it at The Waterside Inn and I never tire of it. It adds an entirely new dimension to a pork pie bought from the delicatessen. At home, I always keep a few jars of pear or peach chutney, which I love to eat with leftover cold roast pheasant or partridge. Most of these sauces are simple to prepare and taste wonderful served with all pâtés and terrines, whether home-made or bought from the charcuterie.

Hot game sauces fill the kitchen with heavenly aromas as they cook. They help to make high or very rich game more digestible. Among my favourites is that all-time great, poivrade sauce, whose satisfying flavour marries well with almost all game. The glowing autumnal colours and fruity flavours of sauces made with figs or port will awaken your appetite. You will also discover that bitter chocolate strays from the confines of desserts into one of these savoury sauces.

ROAST PARTRIDGE
WITH PORT SAUCE
AND APPLE SAUCE

Port Sauce

Sauce au porto

One of my favourite simple game dishes is pan-fried pheasant breasts served with this light sauce. It is also excellent with pan-fried venison cutlets and roast partridge. For preference, I would use blackcurrants, but since their season is short, I also use cranberries. These give the sauce a very slightly bitter tinge which is refreshing and very digestible.

Serves 4
PREPARATION TIME: 10 MINUTES
COOKING TIME: 30 MINUTES

Ingredients:
60G BUTTER
60G SHALLOTS, VERY FINELY SLICED
100G BUTTON MUSHROOMS, FINELY SLICED
50G CRANBERRIES OR BLACKCURRANTS
250ML RED PORT, AT LEAST 10 YEARS OLD
DRIED ZEST OF $1/4$ ORANGE
300ML VEAL STOCK (PAGE 16)
OR GAME STOCK (PAGE 19)
SALT AND FRESHLY GROUND PEPPER

Melt half the butter in a small saucepan. Add the shallots and sweat until soft, then add the mushrooms and cranberries or blackcurrants and cook gently for 3–4 minutes. Pour in the port, add the orange zest and reduce by one-third. Add the stock and simmer for 25 minutes, skimming the surface whenever necessary.

Pass the sauce through a conical sieve, swirl in the rest of the butter, shaking and rotating the pan, then season to taste with salt and pepper.

(Picture page 72)

Apple Sauce

Sauce aux pommes

Apple sauce is delicious served with young wild boar, wild duck, roast partridge and pheasant or roast pork.

Serves 6
PREPARATION TIME: 5 MINUTES
COOKING TIME: ABOUT 15 MINUTES

Ingredients:
500G DESSERT APPLES, PREFERABLY COX
150ML WATER
20G CASTER SUGAR
JUICE OF $1/2$ LEMON
$1/2$ CINNAMON STICK, OR A PINCH OF GROUND
CINNAMON
30G BUTTER
A PINCH OF SALT

Peel and core the apples and dice them finely. Place in a thick-bottomed saucepan together with all the other ingredients except the butter and salt. Set over medium heat, cover and cook for about 15 minutes, until the apples are tender but not dried out. Take the pan off the heat and, with a small whisk, whisk in the butter and a pinch of salt to make a very smooth compote. The consistency of the sauce will vary according to how ripe or green the apples are. If it seems too thick, add a tablespoon of water. Remove the cinnamon stick before serving.

(Picture page 72)

Marinated Cucumber Relish

Concombre mariné au vinaigre

I really enjoy this cucumber relish, which our young protégé Mark Prescott often serves at his pub, The White Hart at Nayland. It is delicious served with fish galantines and terrines or with gravadlax.

Makes 550g
PREPARATION TIME: ABOUT 10 MINUTES,
PLUS 2 HOURS' MARINATING
COOKING TIME: ABOUT 1 HOUR 30 MINUTES

Ingredients:
For the marinated cucumbers
(prepare these 2 hours in advance)
1KG CUCUMBERS
150G ONIONS
1 GREEN PEPPER
1 RED PEPPER
1 RED CHILLI
SALT

For the syrup:
500ML WHITE WINE
300G SOFT LIGHT BROWN SUGAR
A SMALL PINCH OF GROUND CLOVES
1 TSP TURMERIC
2 TSP MUSTARD SEEDS
1 TSP FENNEL SEEDS

Prepare and marinate the cucumbers 2 hours in advance. Leave them unpeeled, but halve them lengthways, scoop out the seeds and slice the flesh very thinly. Peel and finely slice the onions. Peel the green and red peppers, remove the seeds and white membranes and cut the flesh into very fine *julienne*. Cut the chilli into very fine *julienne*. Put everything in a non-metallic bowl, add salt to taste and leave to marinate for 2 hours.

To make the syrup, put all the ingredients in a saucepan and bring slowly to the boil over low heat. Cook for about 45 minutes, until the syrup is thick enough to coat a wooden spoon and your finger leaves a clear trace when you run it down the spoon.

Drain the marinated ingredients, press to eliminate as much liquid as possible, then add them to the syrup. Cook gently for 45 minutes, stirring occasionally with a wooden spoon, until the relish has a soft, melting jam-like consistency. Transfer it to an airtight jar and keep in a cool place until ready to use. It will keep in the fridge for several weeks.

Poivrade Sauce

Sauce poivrade

This sauce should be made with the marinade you have used for the game the sauce is to accompany. Poivrade sauce is rich and powerful and perfect for a large piece of game, such as a haunch of venison, saddle of young wild boar or roast chump of hare. It can also be served with pan-fried noisettes of venison. As these are delicate, you should not swamp the flavour with a very full-bodied sauce, so use only half the given quantity of marinade and do not reduce the sauce too much.

Serves 6
PREPARATION TIME: 20 MINUTES
COOKING TIME: ABOUT 1 HOUR 15 MINUTES

Ingredients:
3 TBSP OIL
500G TRIMMINGS OF FURRED GAME (EG: VENISON,
HARE, WILD BOAR), CUT INTO PIECES
100G CARROTS, CHOPPED
80G ONION, CHOPPED
30ML RED WINE VINEGAR
200ML COOKED MARINADE (PAGE 23)
500ML VEAL STOCK (PAGE 16)
OR GAME STOCK (PAGE 19)
1 BOUQUET GARNI (PAGE 10)
6 PEPPERCORNS, CRUSHED
40G BUTTER, CHILLED AND DICED
SALT AND FRESHLY GROUND PEPPER

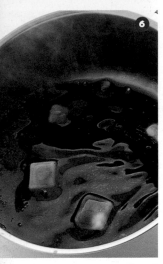

Heat the oil in a deep frying pan, put in the game trimmings (1) and brown them over high heat (2). Strain off the oil and fat released by the cooking, add the chopped carrot and onion to the pan and sweat over low heat for 3 minutes (3). Pour in the vinegar and marinade and cook over medium heat for 5 minutes (4). Add the stock and bouquet garni and cook at a bare simmer for 45 minutes (5), then add the crushed peppercorns and cook for a further 10 minutes.

Strain the sauce through a conical sieve into a small saucepan. Off the heat, swirl in the butter, a little at a time (6), until the sauce is smooth and glossy (7). Season to taste and serve at once, or keep the sauce warm, taking care not to let it boil. If you are going to do this, add the butter only at the last moment.

GRAND VENEUR SAUCE: Add 2 tsp redcurrant jelly and 2 tbsp double cream to the poivrade sauce to make a Grand Veneur Sauce (this means 'Master of the King's Hunt')

Cumberland Sauce

Sauce Cumberland

This sauce miraculously enhances the character of meats and terrines. Serve it cold with galantines and ballotines, pork pies or any poultry or game. The sauce tastes even better the day after it is made.

Serves 4
PREPARATION TIME: 10 MINUTES
COOKING TIME: 20 MINUTES

Ingredients:
1 MEDIUM SHALLOT, FINELY CHOPPED
4 TBSP WINE VINEGAR, PREFERABLY RED
12 WHITE PEPPERCORNS, CRUSHED
100ML VEAL STOCK (PAGE 16)
50ML RUBY PORT
2 TBSP REDCURRANT JELLY
1 TSP WORCESTERSHIRE SAUCE
JUICE OF 1 ORANGE
ZEST OF 1 LEMON, BLANCHED AND
CUT INTO JULIENNE
SALT

COMBINE THE VINEGAR,
SHALLOT AND PEPPERCORNS
IN A PAN AND REDUCE BY
TWO-THIRDS

Combine the shallot, vinegar and peppercorns in a small saucepan and reduce by two-thirds over high heat. Add the veal stock, port, redcurrant jelly, Worcestershire sauce and orange juice, quickly bring to the boil, then lower the heat and simmer gently for 20 minutes. Season with salt.

Pass the sauce through a conical strainer into a bowl, cool, then refrigerate, as the sauce should be served very cold. Just before serving, stir in the lemon zest.

SHRED THE BLANCHED LEMON
ZEST INTO JULIENNE

LEFT: ADD THE PORT TO THE
SAUCE

CUMBERLAND SAUCE TASTES
WONDERFUL WITH ALL MEAT
AND GAME TERRINES

Rich Pomerol Sauce

Sauce riche au vin de Pomerol

This rich, profound and complex sauce is perfect with roast saddle of hare or a well-marinated roast gigot of young wild boar. The perfect accompaniments to these regal game dishes are spätzle noodles, chestnuts and braised celeriac.

Serves 6
PREPARATION TIME: 10 MINUTES
COOKING TIME: ABOUT 25 MINUTES

Ingredients:
300ML TOP QUALITY POMEROL WINE
1 QUANTITY POIVRADE SAUCE (PAGE 76), WITHOUT THE ADDED BUTTER
20G BITTER CHOCOLATE (AT LEAST 70% COCOA SOLIDS), MELTED
75G FOIE GRAS BUTTER (PAGE 63)
SALT AND FRESHLY GROUND PEPPER

Pour the wine into a saucepan and reduce it by one-third. Add the poivrade sauce and simmer gently for 15 minutes, then whisk in the melted chocolate. Bubble the sauce for 30 seconds, then turn off the heat and whisk in the foie gras butter, a little at a time. Pass the sauce through a wire-mesh conical sieve, season with salt and pepper and serve at once.

Pumpkin Sauce with Sweet Spices

Sauce au potiron et aux épices douces

This fruity sauce with its delicate flavour of spices is perfect with fillets of wild rabbit, noisettes of young wild boar or pan-fried breast of wild duck served with a light garlic-flavoured potato purée and crisply cooked mange-tout.

Serves 4
PREPARATION TIME: 20 MINUTES
COOKING TIME: ABOUT 1 1/2 HOURS

Ingredients:
500G GAME TRIMMINGS OR CHOPPED GAME CARCASSES
3 TBSP OIL
60G SHALLOTS, FINELY CHOPPED
300G PUMPKIN FLESH, CUT INTO SMALL CUBES
50ML RASPBERRY VINEGAR, HOME-MADE (PAGE 44) OR BOUGHT
200ML SWEET WHITE WINE (SAUTERNES OR BARSAC)
500ML VEGETABLE STOCK (PAGE 22)
1 BOUQUET GARNI (PAGE 10)
1 VANILLA POD, SPLIT LENGTHWAYS
3 STAR ANISE
40G BUTTER, WELL CHILLED AND DICED
SALT AND FRESHLY GROUND PEPPER

Heat the oil in a deep frying pan, add the game trimmings or carcasses and briskly brown them all over. Pour off the oil and fat released by the game, then put in the shallots and pumpkin and sweat them gently over low heat for 3 minutes. Turn off the heat and add the raspberry vinegar. After 1 minute, deglaze with the white wine and simmer for 5 minutes, then add the vegetable stock, bouquet garni and spices and cook very gently for 45 minutes, skimming the surface whenever necessary.

Pass the sauce through a wire-mesh conical sieve into a clean pan and reduce until it coats the back of a spoon. Off the heat, whisk in the butter, a little at a time. Season to taste with salt and pepper and serve the sauce at once.

Arabica Fig Sauce

Sauces aux figues arabica

This sauce is excellent with roast wild duck or wood pigeon. Fresh figs poached in red wine make a wonderful garnish. Be careful not to boil the sauce after adding the coffee, or it will become slightly bitter.

Serves 8
PREPARATION TIME: 10 MINUTES
COOKING TIME: ABOUT 40 MINUTES

Ingredients:
6 VERY RIPE FRESH FIGS, EACH
CUT INTO 6 PIECES
100ML RUBY PORT
400ML GAME STOCK (PAGE 19)
6 BLACK PEPPERCORNS, CRUSHED
1 TBSP INSTANT COFFEE POWDER, DISSOLVED
IN 1 TBSP WATER
40G BUTTER, CHILLED AND DICED
SALT AND FRESHLY GROUND PEPPER

Put the figs and port in a saucepan and simmer gently for 5 minutes. Pour in the game stock, add the crushed peppercorns and bubble gently for 25 minutes, skimming the surface from time to time. Add the coffee, then immediately turn off the heat.

Pour the sauce into a blender, whizz for 30 seconds, then pass it through a wire-mesh conical sieve and whisk in the butter, one piece at a time. Season to taste with salt and pepper and serve immediately.

Peach Chutney

Chutney aux pêches

Make this chutney in summer, when peaches are fresh and cheap. It is delicious served with terrines and pâtés, cold meats, and especially with cold chicken for a picnic.

Makes about 700g
PREPARATION TIME: 25 MINUTES
COOKING TIME: ABOUT 1 HOUR 10 MINUTES

Ingredients:
500G PEACHES, PREFERABLY YELLOW, PEELED,
STONED AND ROUGHLY CUT INTO LARGE DICE
60G COOKING APPLE, PEELED AND GRATED
1/2 TSP SALT
125G VERY RIPE TOMATOES, PEELED,
DESEEDED AND CHOPPED
60G ONION, FINELY CHOPPED
ZEST OF 1 LIME, FINELY CHOPPED
JUICE OF THE LIME
150G CASTER SUGAR
1/2 TSP GROUND CINNAMON
1/2 TSP GROUND NUTMEG
1/2 TSP GROUND WHITE PEPPER
1 GARLIC CLOVE, CRUSHED
10G FRESH GINGER, FINELY CHOPPED
150ML WHITE WINE VINEGAR
70G FLAKED ALMONDS

Combine all the ingredients except the peaches in a thick-bottomed saucepan and bring to the boil over very low heat, stirring from time to time with a wooden spoon. Continue to cook for about 30 minutes, giving a stir every 10 minutes, until the mixture is jam-like and syrupy. Test by wiping your finger down the back of the spoon; it should leave a clear trace.

Add the peaches and cook very gently for another 40 minutes, stirring every 10 minutes. Transfer the chutney to a 750ml kilner jar, leave to cool completely, then seal the jar. Keep in the fridge until needed (it will keep for several weeks).

Pear Chutney

Chutney aux poires

This chutney is best left for a few days before you eat it. Serve it with cold meats, terrines, pâtés and game, or simply spread on a slice of toast.

Makes about 600g
PREPARATION TIME: 30 MINUTES
COOKING TIME: ABOUT 1 HOUR 50 MINUTES

Ingredients:
375G PEARS, PEELED, CORED AND CUT INTO LARGE DICE
60G COOKING APPLE, PEELED AND CHOPPED
1/2 TSP SALT
125G VERY RIPE TOMATOES, PEELED, DESEEDED AND CHOPPED
60G ONION, FINELY CHOPPED
60G SULTANAS
1 TBSP ORANGE ZEST, COARSELY CHOPPED
JUICE OF 1 ORANGE
150G CASTER SUGAR
1/4 TSP GROUND CINNAMON
1/4 TSP GROUND NUTMEG
1/4 TSP CAYENNE PEPPER
15G FRESH GINGER, FINELY CHOPPED
150ML WHITE WINE VINEGAR
A PINCH OF SAFFRON POWDER OR THREADS

Combine all the ingredients except the pears in a thick-bottomed saucepan and bring to the boil over very low heat, stirring from time to time with a wooden spoon. Continue to cook for about 1 hour, giving a stir every 10 minutes, until the mixture is jam-like and syrupy. Test by wiping your finger down the back of the spoon; it should leave a clear trace.

Add the pears and cook very gently for another 40 minutes, stirring every 10 minutes. Transfer the chutney to a 500ml kilner jar, leave to cool completely, then seal the jar. Keep in the fridge until needed (it will keep for several weeks).

INGREDIENTS FOR PEAR CHUTNEY

BOIL ALL THE INGREDIENTS EXCEPT THE PEARS FOR ABOUT 1 HOUR

THE MIXTURE SHOULD HAVE THE CONSISTENCY OF JAM

ADD THE PEARS TO THE MIXTURE

COOK THE CHUTNEY FOR ANOTHER 40 MINUTES, STIRRING EVERY 10 MINUTES

RIGHT: USE A FUNNEL TO TRANSFER THE CHUTNEY TO A KILNER JAR

Venison Sauce with Blackberries

Sauce chevreuil aux mûres

This fragrant, satisfying but not overly-rich sauce is ideal with a roast saddle or gigot of venison, especially in the autumn and winter months.

Serves 6
PREPARATION TIME: 10 MINUTES
COOKING TIME: ABOUT 40 MINUTES

Ingredients:
150G BLACKBERRIES
30G CASTER SUGAR
2 TBSP RED WINE VINEGAR
600ML GAME STOCK (PAGE 19)
DRIED ZEST OF $1/2$ ORANGE
$1/2$ CINNAMON STICK
50ML BANYULS WINE
60G BUTTER, WELL CHILLED AND DICED
SALT AND FRESHLY GROUND PEPPER

Put the blackberries and sugar in a saucepan and cook over low heat, stirring with a wooden spoon until the blackberries have collapsed into a purée. Turn off the heat, add the vinegar, give a stir, then pour in the game stock. Add the dried orange zest and cinnamon, bring to the boil, then simmer gently for 25 minutes, skimming the surface whenever necessary. Add the wine and cook for a further 5 minutes, then pass the sauce through a wire-mesh conical sieve into another saucepan. Whisk in the butter, a little at a time, season the sauce with salt and pepper and serve at once.

Vineyard Sauce with Five Spices

Sauce vigneronne aux cinque épices

For a delicious main course, serve this sauce with roast pheasant or partridge garnished with peeled and deseeded grapes. If you prefer a less pronounced gamey flavour, substitute veal stock for the game stock.

Serves 6
PREPARATION TIME: 15 MINUTES
COOKING TIME: ABOUT 45 MINUTES

Ingredients:
24 GRAPES, PEELED AND DESEEDED
50G CASTER SUGAR
50ML ARMAGNAC OR COGNAC
300ML RED WINE, PREFERABLY CÔTES DU RHÔNE
500ML GAME STOCK (PAGE 19)
1 TSP FIVE-SPICE POWDER
1 SMALL BOUQUET GARNI (PAGE 10),
INCLUDING 2 SAGE LEAVES
50G BUTTER, WELL CHILLED AND DICED
SALT AND FRESHLY GROUND PEPPER

Put the grapes and sugar in a saucepan, set over medium heat and cook, stirring every minute with a wooden spoon, until the grapes have disintegrated into a lightly caramelized compote. Add the Armagnac or Cognac and ignite it, then pour in the wine and cook until it has reduced by one-third.

Add all the other ingredients and simmer for 30 minutes, or until the sauce is thick enough to coat the back of a spoon, skimming the surface whenever necessary. Pass the sauce through a wire-mesh conical sieve, season with salt and pepper, then whisk in the chilled butter, a little at a time. Serve immediately.

Quick Sauce
for Game Birds

Sauce minute pour gibier à plumes

This quickly-prepared but serious sauce is not too robust, but since it absorbs the savour of the carcasses during its brief cooking, it retains the full flavour of the game birds.

Serves 4
PREPARATION TIME: 5 MINUTES
COOKING TIME: ABOUT 30 MINUTES

Ingredients:
2 WILD DUCK, OR 2 SNIPE, OR 4 WOOD PIGEONS
50ML COGNAC OR ARMAGNAC
150ML RED WINE
450ML VEGETABLE STOCK (PAGE 22)
5 JUNIPER BERRIES, CRUSHED
1 SPRIG OF THYME
1/2 BAY LEAF
4 TBSP DOUBLE CREAM
SALT AND FRESHLY GROUND PEPPER

Roast the game birds until they are cooked to your liking, then remove the thighs and breasts, wrap them in foil and keep them warm until ready to eat.

Chop the carcasses, place in a saucepan and heat them through, then add the Armagnac or Cognac and ignite it. Pour in the red wine and reduce it by half over high heat, then add the vegetable stock, juniper berries, thyme and bay leaf. Cook briskly to reduce the liquid by half, add the cream and bubble for another 3 minutes. Pass the sauce through a wire-mesh conical sieve, season with salt and pepper and serve immediately with the reserved breast and thigh meat.

Cranberry
and Bilberry Sauce

Sauce aux airelles et myrtilles

I serve this sauce with terrines of game or pâtés en croûte. It is also good served just warm with wild roast goose. The berries, particularly bilberries, can sometimes be rather tart; if so, add about 30g caster sugar to the sauce halfway through cooking.

Serves 8
PREPARATION TIME: 5 MINUTES
COOKING TIME: ABOUT 30 MINUTES

Ingredients:
150G CRANBERRIES
75G CASTER SUGAR
1 CLOVE, CRUSHED
150G BILBERRIES
200ML COLD WATER
JUICE OF 1 LEMON
ZEST OF THE LEMON, CUT INTO
JULIENNE AND BLANCHED

Put the cranberries in a saucepan, add 100 ml cold water, then the sugar and clove and cook gently for 10 minutes. Add the bilberries, the remaining cold water and the lemon juice and simmer for 20 minutes. Keep the sauce at room temperature; it should not be served too cold. If you prefer a very smooth sauce with no fruit skins, pass it through a strainer. Stir in the lemon zest just before serving.

CHAPTER 6

These sauces should be delicate and light; their flavour should harmonize with the seafood they accompany and never dominate it. This is particularly important in the case of white fish.

Sauces for Fish & Shellfish

I like to serve fish with a nage, a light, aromatic stock, to which I sometimes add just a tiny soupçon of fresh herbs, like snipped chervil, basil or tarragon. I prefer my fish barely cooked, so that it remains juicy. The sauce should be there to bring out the fresh, salty tang and the delicate flavour of the sea, adding extra pleasure to the palate.

In contrast, sauces for crustaceans should be flavoured with stronger herbs and spices to give them a more defined edge and character.

Sauces for fish and seafood often contain dry white wine; variations include beer, Champagne, vermouth or even a sweet Sauternes.

TAGLIATELLE AND SEAFOOD SAUCE
WITH SAFFRON

Seafood Sauce with Saffron

Sauce aux fruits de mer safranée

This is the perfect sauce for any lightly poached seafood, langoustines or lobster, or for fresh flat pasta.

Serves 4
PREPARATION TIME: 10 MINUTES
COOKING TIME: ABOUT 20 MINUTES

Ingredients:
350ML COOKING JUICES FROM SHELLFISH, SUCH
AS MUSSELS, SCALLOPS, OYSTERS, CLAMS ETC
250ML FISH STOCK (PAGE 21), OR COOKING JUICES
FROM LANGOUSTINES
A PINCH OF SAFFRON THREADS
200ML DOUBLE CREAM
SALT AND FRESHLY GROUND WHITE PEPPER

Combine the shellfish juices and fish stock in a saucepan, set over high heat and reduce by two-thirds. Add the saffron and cream and bubble for 5 minutes, until the sauce will lightly coat the back of a spoon. Pass it through a conical sieve and season to taste.

For a less calorific sauce, you can substitute fromage frais for the double cream, but do not allow the sauce to boil. Heat it to 90°C and whisk well before serving, or, better still, give it a quick whizz in a blender.

(Picture page 86)

Claret Sauce

Sauce lie de vin

This vinous, characterful sauce is traditionally made with the dregs or 'lees' at the bottom of the bottle. Serve it as a base for pink-fleshed fish, such as salmon, red mullet or tuna escalopes. Pan-fry the fish at the last moment, pour the sauce on to the plate and place the fish on top.

Serves 8
PREPARATION TIME: 5 MINUTES
COOKING TIME: ABOUT 40 MINUTES

Ingredients:
300ML FULL-BODIED RED WINE,
PREFERABLY CLARET
200ML VEAL STOCK (PAGE 16)
300ML FISH STOCK (PAGE 21), MADE
WITH RED WINE
50G SHALLOTS, FINELY SLICED
60G BUTTON MUSHROOMS, FINELY SLICED
I SMALL BOUQUET GARNI (PAGE 10)
50ML DOUBLE CREAM
200G BUTTER, CHILLED AND DICED
SALT AND FRESHLY GROUND PEPPER

Combine all the ingredients except the cream and butter in a saucepan, set over medium heat and reduce until slightly syrupy. Remove the bouquet garni, add the cream and give the sauce a good bubble, then strain it through a conical sieve into a clean saucepan. Whisk in the butter, a small piece at a time, until the sauce is rich and glossy. Season to taste and serve hot.

Nantua Sauce

Sauce Nantua

An excellent sauce for langoustines, scallops and any white fish with delicate, firm flesh. A tablespoon of snipped tarragon added just before serving will make it taste even better.

Serves 8
PREPARATION TIME: 20 MINUTES
COOKING TIME: ABOUT 50 MINUTES

Ingredients:
120G BUTTER
60G SHALLOTS, VERY FINELY SLICED
60G BUTTON MUSHROOMS, VERY FINELY SLICED
16 CRAYFISH OR LANGOUSTINE HEADS, RAW OR COOKED, ROUGHLY CHOPPED
2 TBSP COGNAC
150ML DRY WHITE WINE
300ML FISH STOCK (PAGE 21)
1 SMALL BOUQUET GARNI (PAGE 10), INCLUDING A SPRIG OR TWO OF TARRAGON
80G RIPE TOMATOES, PEELED AND DESEEDED
A PINCH OF CAYENNE PEPPER
300ML DOUBLE CREAM
SALT AND FRESHLY GROUND PEPPER

In a shallow saucepan, melt 40g butter over low heat. Add the chopped shallots and mushrooms and sweat for 1 minute. Add the crayfish or langoustine heads to the pan, increase the heat and fry briskly for 2–3 minutes, stirring continuously with a spatula.

Pour in the Cognac, ignite with a match, add the wine and reduce by half, then pour in the fish stock. Bring to the boil, then lower the heat so that the sauce bubbles gently. Add the bouquet garni, tomato, cayenne and a smidgeon of salt and cook for 30 minutes.

Stir in the cream and bubble the sauce for another 10 minutes. Remove the bouquet garni, transfer the contents of the pan to a food processor and whizz for 2 minutes. Strain the sauce through a fine-mesh conical sieve into a clean saucepan, rubbing it through with the back of a ladle. Bring the sauce back to the boil and season with salt and pepper. Off the heat, whisk in the remaining butter, a little at a time, until the sauce is smooth and glossy. It is now ready to serve.

Champagne Sauce

Sauce Champagne

This sauce is perfect for poached white fish, such as John Dory, turbot or sole. You can substitute sparkling white wine for the Champagne, but the sauce will not taste as good.

Serves 8
PREPARATION TIME: 10 MINUTES
COOKING TIME: ABOUT 50 MINUTES

Ingredients:
50G BUTTER
60G SHALLOTS, VERY FINELY SLICED
60G BUTTON MUSHROOMS, FINELY SLICED
400ML BRUT CHAMPAGNE
300ML FISH STOCK (PAGE 21)
500ML DOUBLE CREAM
SALT AND FRESHLY GROUND WHITE PEPPER

In a saucepan, melt 20g butter. Add the chopped shallots and sweat them for 1 minute, without colouring. Add the mushrooms and cook for a further 2 minutes, stirring continuously with a wooden spatula. Pour in the Champagne and reduce by one-third over medium heat. Add the fish stock and reduce the sauce by half.

Pour in the cream and reduce the sauce until it lightly coats the back of a spoon. Pass it through a fine-mesh conical sieve into a clean pan. Whisk in the remaining butter, a little at a time, then season the sauce with salt and pepper.

For a lighter texture, whizz the sauce in a food processor for 1 minute before serving.

Américaine Sauce

Sauce américaine

This classic 'star' sauce should be eaten with a spoon. It takes time to prepare, but is worth the effort. Serve it with firm-fleshed fish, such as poached turbot, or a turbot soufflé homardine.

Serves 6
PREPARATION TIME: 40 MINUTES
COOKING TIME: ABOUT 1 HOUR

Ingredients:
1 LIVE LOBSTER, 800G–1KG
100ML GROUNDNUT OIL
4 TBSP VERY FINELY DICED CARROTS
2 TBSP VERY FINELY DICED SHALLOT OR ONION
2 GARLIC CLOVES, UNPEELED AND CRUSHED
50ML COGNAC OR ARMAGNAC
300ML DRY WHITE WINE
300ML FISH STOCK (PAGE 21)
200G VERY RIPE TOMATOES, PEELED, DESEEDED AND CHOPPED
1 BOUQUET GARNI (PAGE 10), CONTAINING A SPRIG OF TARRAGON
60G BUTTER
10G FLOUR
A SMALL PINCH OF CAYENNE PEPPER
75ML DOUBLE CREAM (OPTIONAL)
SALT AND FRESHLY GROUND PEPPER

ABOVE AND BELOW: SEPARATE THE HEAD AND THE BODY AND CUT THE CLAW JOINTS AND TAIL INTO RINGS

SPLIT THE HEAD AND REMOVE THE GRITTY SAC

Bring a large pan of water to the boil. Rinse the lobster under cold running water and plunge it into the boiling water for 45 seconds. Separate the head and body and cut the claw joints and tail into rings across the articulations. Split the head lengthways and remove the gritty sac close to the feelers, and the dirty white membranes. Scrape out the greenish coral from inside the head and reserve in a bowl. Season the lobster with cayenne, salt and pepper.

In a deep frying pan or shallow saucepan, heat the oil over high heat. As soon as it is sizzling hot, add all the lobster pieces (1) and sauté until the shell turns bright red and the flesh is lightly coloured (2). Remove the lobster pieces with a slotted spoon and place on a plate. Discard most of the cooking oil.

Using the same pan, sweat the carrot and shallot until soft but not coloured. Add the garlic (3), return the lobster pieces to the pan, pour in the Cognac (4)

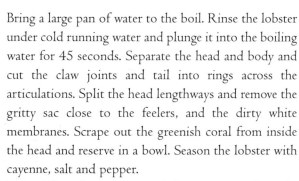

SCRAPE OUT THE GREENISH CORAL FROM INSIDE THE HEAD AND RESERVE

1 2
3 4

REMOVE THE
LOBSTER CLAWS
AND TAIL RINGS
AND RESERVE

and light with a match. Add the wine and fish stock, then add the tomatoes, bouquet garni and a touch of salt. As soon as the mixture comes to the boil, lower the heat and cook gently for 15 minutes. Remove and reserve the claws and rings of lobster tail containing the meat. Cook the sauce at a gentle bubble for a further 30 minutes, skimming it every 15 minutes.

Using a fork, mash together the reserved lobster coral, butter and flour, and add this mixture to the sauce, a little at a time. Cook for another 5 minutes, then add the cream if you wish and pass the sauce through a fine-mesh conical strainer, pressing it through with the back of a ladle. Season with salt and pepper. For a lighter texture, whizz the sauce in a food processor for 1 minute. Remove the reserved lobster meat from the shell, dice it and add to the sauce just before serving.

ADD THE CREAM
(OPTIONAL)

ADD THE LOBSTER
CORAL, BUTTER AND
FLOUR MIXTURE

RIGHT: PASS THE SAUCE
THROUGH A SIEVE, PRESSING
WITH THE BACK OF A LADLE

Thermidor Sauce

Sauce thermidor

This famous companion to lobster thermidor is sadly often poorly made and therefore disappointing. I enjoy it with almost all crustaceans, especially mixed with crabmeat and served au gratin. *If you wish, add a teaspoon of Cognac to the sauce at the end of cooking.*

Serves 6
PREPARATION TIME: 10 MINUTES
COOKING TIME: ABOUT 40 MINUTES

Ingredients:
40G SHALLOT, VERY FINELY CHOPPED
200ML FISH STOCK (PAGE 21)
200ML DRY WHITE WINE
300ML BÉCHAMEL SAUCE (PAGE 128)
100ML DOUBLE CREAM
1 TSP STRONG DIJON MUSTARD
1 TSP ENGLISH MUSTARD POWDER, DISSOLVED IN A
FEW DROPS OF WATER
50G BUTTER, WELL CHILLED AND DICED
1 TBSP FINELY SNIPPED TARRAGON
SALT AND CAYENNE PEPPER

Combine the shallot, fish stock and wine in a saucepan and reduce the liquid by two-thirds. Add the béchamel and cook the sauce over low heat for 20 minutes, stirring every 5 minutes. Pour in the cream, bubble for 5 minutes, then add both mustards and cook for another 2 minutes. Turn off the heat and whisk the butter into the sauce, one piece at a time. Season with salt and a good pinch of cayenne. Finally add the tarragon and serve immediately.

Mango Sauce

Sauce à la mangue

This refreshing, fruity sauce is perfect for outdoor eating in summer. It is excellent with grilled or barbecued fish or with crustaceans such as lobster or langoustines.

Serves 6
PREPARATION TIME: 10 MINUTES
COOKING TIME: ABOUT 40 MINUTES

Ingredients:
1 MANGO, ABOUT 250G
50ML COGNAC OR ARMAGNAC
A SMALL PINCH OF CURRY POWDER
7G SOFT GREEN PEPPERCORNS, WELL DRAINED
300ML FISH STOCK (PAGE 21)
200ML DOUBLE CREAM
100G PLAIN YOGHURT
1 TBSP SNIPPED FLAT-LEAF PARSLEY
SALT AND FRESHLY GROUND PEPPER

Using a knife with a fine blade, peel the mango and cut away the flesh from around the stone. Put the flesh in a saucepan with the Cognac or Armagnac, curry and green peppercorns and simmer over low heat for 5 minutes. Pour in the fish stock and bubble gently for 20 minutes. Add the cream and cook for another 5 minutes, then turn off the heat and add the yoghurt.

Transfer the sauce to a blender and whizz for 30 seconds, then pass it through a wire-mesh conical sieve and season to taste with salt and pepper. Serve the sauce immediately, or keep it warm (but not too hot) in a bain-marie. Stir in the parsley just before serving.

Watercress Sauce

Sauce cressonnière

A tasty sauce to serve with grilled scallops or lightly-poached oysters. It is extremely light, almost like a bouillon, and should be eaten with a spoon.

Serves 8
PREPARATION TIME: ABOUT 25 MINUTES
COOKING TIME: ABOUT 25 MINUTES

Ingredients:
400G VERY GREEN WATERCRESS
100G BUTTER
500ML VEGETABLE STOCK (PAGE 22)
15G SOFT GREEN PEPPERCORNS
SALT AND FRESHLY GROUND PEPPER

Cut off and discard most of the watercress stalks. In a saucepan, melt 30g of the butter. Add the watercress and sweat it over low heat for 3 minutes, stirring continuously with a spatula.

Add the vegetable stock and green peppercorns, increase the heat to high and cook for 10 minutes. Turn off the heat and leave the sauce to infuse for 10 minutes, then pour it into a food processor and whizz for 2 minutes. Pass the sauce through a fine-mesh conical sieve into a clean saucepan, rubbing it through with the back of a ladle. Reheat until bubbling, then take the pan off the heat and whisk in the remaining butter, a little at a time. Season with salt and pepper.

Tomato Nage

Nage de tomates

This light nage *is perfect with lightly poached crustaceans, or grilled fish such as escalope of salmon or fillets of sole. It can be enhanced with a little snipped basil added at the last moment. If fresh tomatoes are slightly lacking in flavour, add a teaspoon of tomato purée.*

Serves 8
PREPARATION TIME: 15 MINUTES
COOKING TIME: 25 MINUTES

Ingredients:
350G VERY RIPE TOMATOES, PEELED,
DESEEDED AND CHOPPED
50G SHALLOTS, FINELY SLICED
50G BUTTON MUSHROOMS, FINELY SLICED
1 SPRIG OF THYME
1 BAY LEAF
250ML VEGETABLE STOCK (PAGE 22)
A PINCH OF SUGAR
50ML DOUBLE CREAM
250G BUTTER
SALT AND FRESHLY GROUND PEPPER

Combine all the ingredients except the cream and butter in a saucepan and bring to the boil over medium heat. As soon as the mixture starts to bubble, lower the heat and reduce the liquid by two-thirds. Now add the cream and bubble the sauce for 3 minutes. Off the heat, whisk in the butter, a little at a time. Strain the sauce through a fine-mesh conical sieve into a clean saucepan and season to taste. The *nage* is now ready to use.

Shrimp Sauce

Sauce aux crevettes

This is delicious with almost all poached, steamed or braised fish. I also love it poured over quartered hard-boiled eggs. I sometimes add a couple of tablespoons of dry sherry to the sauce just before serving.

Serves 6
PREPARATION TIME: 15 MINUTES
COOKING TIME: ABOUT 45 MINUTES

Ingredients:
600ML FISH STOCK, COOLED (PAGE 21)
40G BLOND ROUX, HOT (PAGE 33)
200ML DOUBLE CREAM
60G SHRIMP BUTTER (PAGE 61)
60G COOKED AND PEELED PINK OR BROWN
SHRIMP TAILS
A PINCH OF CAYENNE PEPPER
SALT AND FRESHLY GROUND PEPPER

Put the hot roux in a saucepan, set over medium heat and whisk in the cold fish stock. As soon as it comes to the boil, reduce the heat to very low and cook gently for 30 minutes, whisking every 10 minutes and making sure that the whisk goes right into the bottom of the pan. Use a spoon to remove any skin which forms on this *velouté* as it cooks.

After 30 minutes, add the cream and bubble the sauce for another 10 minutes. Reduce the heat to the lowest possible (use a heat diffuser if you have one) and whisk in the shrimp butter, a little at a time. Season the sauce with salt and pepper and spice it up with cayenne to taste. Pass it through a wire-mesh conical sieve, then add the shrimp tails and serve immediately.

Fish Fumet with Tomatoes and Basil

Fumet de poissons à la tomate et au basilic

Steamed fillets of fish with delicate flesh such as red mullet, John Dory or sea bream are delicious served in a deep plate, bathed with a ladle of this fat-free, summery fumet, *redolent with the aromas of tomatoes and basil. If you wish, sprinkle over some very finely shredded basil.*

Serves 6
PREPARATION TIME: 5 MINUTES
COOKING TIME: ABOUT 30 MINUTES

Ingredients:
600ML FISH STOCK (PAGE 21)

For the clarification:
500G VERY RIPE TOMATOES, CHOPPED
1 SMALL RED PEPPER, WHITE MEMBRANES AND SEEDS
REMOVED, VERY THINLY SLICED
50G BASIL, COARSELY CHOPPED
4 EGG WHITES
8 PEPPERCORNS, CRUSHED
SALT AND FRESHLY GROUND PEPPER

Mix the clarification ingredients together very thoroughly. Pour the fish stock into a saucepan and add the clarification mixture. Bring to the boil over medium heat, stirring every 5 minutes with a wooden spoon. As soon as the liquid boils, reduce the heat and bubble very gently for 20 minutes. Pass the clarified *fumet* through a wire-mesh conical sieve, season with salt and pepper and serve.

Curried Mussel Sauce

Sauce mouclade d'Aunis

This sauce accompanies to perfection mussels cooked à la marinière and taken out of their shells, or poached cod or halibut. It is also wonderful with a rice pilaff or a dish of pasta bows.

Serves 6
PREPARATION TIME: 5 MINUTES
COOKING TIME: ABOUT 25 MINUTES

Ingredients:
50G BUTTER
60G ONIONS, FINELY CHOPPED
15G FLOUR
2 TSP CURRY POWDER
500ML COOKING JUICES FROM MUSSELS
AND OTHER SHELLFISH, SUCH AS CLAMS
1 SMALL BOUQUET GARNI (PAGE 10)
150ML DOUBLE CREAM
SALT AND FRESHLY GROUND PEPPER

Melt the butter in a saucepan, add the onions and sweat over low heat for 3 minutes. Add the curry powder and flour, stir with a wooden spoon and cook for another 3 minutes, then pour in the cold shellfish juices. Put in the bouquet garni, bring to the boil and leave the sauce to bubble very gently for 20 minutes, stirring with the wooden spoon every 5 minutes. Add the cream, give another bubble, then discard the bouquet garni and season the sauce with salt and pepper. Serve immediately.

ADD THE CURRY POWDER
TO THE SWEATED ONIONS

ADD THE FLOUR AND
STIR IT IN

CURRIED MUSSEL SAUCE
CAN BE MADE WITH
THE JUICES FROM
OTHER SHELLFISH,
SUCH AS CLAMS

ADD THE CREAM TO
THE SAUCE

REMOVE THE
BOUQUET GARNI

Bercy Sauce

Sauce Bercy

This simple, classic sauce goes well with any red- or white-fleshed fish. I enjoy it served with an unusual fish, roussette (dogfish) and also with skate.

Serves 6
PREPARATION TIME: 10 MINUTES
COOKING TIME: ABOUT 35 MINUTES

Ingredients:
60G BUTTER
60G SHALLOTS, VERY FINELY CHOPPED
200ML DRY WHITE WINE
150ML FISH STOCK (PAGE 21)
400ML FISH VELOUTÉ (PAGE 21)
JUICE OF $1/2$ LEMON
2 TBSP CHOPPED PARSLEY
SALT AND FRESHLY GROUND PEPPER

Melt 20g butter in a saucepan, add the chopped shallots and sweat them gently for 1 minute. Pour in the wine and fish stock and cook over medium heat until the liquid has reduced by half. Add the fish *velouté* and simmer gently for 20 minutes. The sauce should be thick enough to coat the back of a spoon lightly. If it is not, cook it for a further 5–10 minutes.

Turn off the heat and whisk in the remaining butter and the lemon juice. Season the sauce, stir in the chopped parsley and serve immediately.

TARRAGON BERCY: Replace the parsley with half the quantity of snipped tarragon to make a tarragon Bercy.

Parsley Nage with Lemon Grass

Nage de persil à la citronnelle

This light, fresh sauce has a gentle lemony flavour underlying the delicious aroma of parsley. Serve it with any poached or pan-fried fish, or with scallops and langoustines.

Serves 6
PREPARATION TIME: 10 MINUTES
COOKING TIME: ABOUT 30 MINUTES

Ingredients:
100G FLAT-LEAF PARSLEY, STALKS AND LEAVES
COARSELY CHOPPED
30G SHALLOT, CHOPPED
1 LEMON GRASS STALK, SPLIT LENGTHWAYS
300ML FISH STOCK (PAGE 21)
OR VEGETABLE STOCK (PAGE 22)
4 TBSP DOUBLE CREAM
JUICE OF $1/2$ LEMON
200G BUTTER, CHILLED AND DICED
2 TBSP FINELY SNIPPED PARSLEY LEAVES
SALT AND FRESHLY GROUND PEPPER

Put the chopped parsley, shallot, lemon grass and stock in a saucepan and cook very gently for 10 minutes. Remove the lemon grass, transfer the contents of the pan to a blender and purée for 1 minute.

Pass the purée through a wire-mesh conical sieve into a clean saucepan, add the cream and lemon juice and bring to the boil. Bubble until the sauce is just thick enough to coat the back of a spoon very lightly. Reduce the heat to as low as possible and incorporate the butter, a little at a time, whisking continuously. Season the sauce to taste with salt and pepper, stir in the finely snipped parsley and serve at once.

Mandarin Sauce

Sauce à la mandarine

This sauce glows with colour and warmth and is particularly good in autumn or winter. Its delicious gentle flavour makes it ideal with poached white-fleshed fish. I serve it with paupiettes of sole, simply poached or filled with a lobster mousse.

Serves 4
PREPARATION TIME: 7 MINUTES
COOKING TIME: ABOUT 20 MINUTES

Ingredients:
250G PEELED MANDARINS, SEGMENTED
150ML FISH STOCK (PAGE 21)
150ML DOUBLE CREAM
2 TBSP Napoleon mandarine LIQUEUR OR GRAND MARNIER
ZEST OF 1 MANDARIN, CUT INTO JULIENNE AND BLANCHED (OPTIONAL)
60G BUTTER, CHILLED AND DICED
SALT AND FRESHLY GROUND PEPPER

Put the mandarin segments in a food processor, mix to a pulp and rub through a fine-mesh sieve. Pour the resulting mandarin juice and the fish stock into a small saucepan, set over medium heat and reduce by half. Add the cream and liqueur and bubble the sauce for a few minutes, until it lightly coats the back of a spoon. Pass it again through the conical sieve. Off the heat, whisk in the butter, a little at a time, to make a smooth shiny sauce. Season to taste, then add the mandarin zest if you wish. Serve at once.

PAUPIETTES OF SOLE FILLED WITH LOBSTER MOUSSE, SERVED WITH MANDARIN SAUCE

POUR THE BEER OVER THE AROMATICS

REDUCE THE LIQUID BY
TWO-THIRDS, ADD THE CREAM
THEN REDUCE UNTIL THE
SAUCE IS THICK ENOUGH TO
COAT THE BACK OF A SPOON

Beer Sauce

Sauce à la bière

This sauce is excellent with braised fish steaks, like turbot or huss. The addition of a spoonful of the braising liquid just before serving will enhance the flavour of the sauce.

Serves 4
PREPARATION TIME: 5 MINUTES
COOKING TIME: ABOUT 15 MINUTES

Ingredients:
60G SHALLOTS, VERY FINELY SLICED
1 SMALL BOUQUET GARNI (PAGE 10)
4 JUNIPER BERRIES, CRUSHED
300ML MILD LIGHT BEER
200ML DOUBLE CREAM
60G BUTTER, CHILLED AND DICED
1/2 TBSP FINELY SNIPPED FLAT-LEAF PARSLEY
SALT AND FRESHLY GROUND PEPPER

Put the shallots, bouquet garni and juniper berries in a saucepan, pour in the beer and reduce by two-thirds over medium heat. Add the cream and bubble for 5 minutes, until the sauce will lightly coat the back of a spoon. If it seems too thin, cook it for a few more minutes. Pass the sauce through a conical sieve, whisk in the butter, a small piece at a time, and finally stir in the parsley. Season to taste with salt and pepper.

WHISK IN THE BUTTER

SWIRL THE PARSLEY INTO THE BEER SAUCE

Vermouth Sauce

Sauce minute au Noilly

We used to serve this sauce with a cassolette of scallops when we first opened our restaurant Le Gavroche. It is still hugely popular with our customers and I often serve it at The Waterside Inn with braised white fish.

Serves 4
PREPARATION TIME: 5 MINUTES
COOKING TIME: ABOUT 20 MINUTES

Ingredients:
40G SHALLOT, FINELY CHOPPED
1 SPRIG OF THYME
1/2 BAY LEAF
100ML NOILLY PRAT OR DRY VERMOUTH
300ML FISH STOCK (PAGE 21)
2 TBSP DOUBLE CREAM
A PINCH OF PAPRIKA
60G BUTTER, WELL CHILLED AND DICED
SALT AND FRESHLY GROUND PEPPER

Put the shallot, thyme, bay leaf and vermouth in a saucepan and reduce by one-third over high heat. Pour in the fish stock and cook over medium heat for 10 minutes, then add the cream. Reduce the sauce over high heat until it is thick enough to coat the back of a spoon. Remove the thyme and bay leaf, whisk in the paprika and turn the heat down to low, making sure that the sauce does not boil. Whisk in the butter, a little at a time, then season with salt and pepper.

Transfer the sauce to a blender, whizz for 30 seconds until foamy and serve immediately.

Sauternes Sauce with Pistachios

Sauce au Sauternes et aux pistaches

I like to serve this sauce with poached or steamed fillets of sole, salmon, sea bass, turbot or John Dory. Depending on the fish, I sometimes add some freshly skinned and chopped pistachios to the sauce just before serving.

Serves 6
PREPARATION TIME: 10 MINUTES
COOKING TIME: ABOUT 40 MINUTES

Ingredients:
20G BUTTER
150G BUTTON MUSHROOMS, THINLY SLICED
300 ML SWEET WHITE WINE (SAUTERNES OR BARSAC)
600ML FISH STOCK (PAGE 21)
75G BLOND ROUX (PAGE 33), COOLED
80G PISTACHIO BUTTER (PAGE 57)
150ML DOUBLE CREAM
SALT AND FRESHLY GROUND PEPPER

Melt the butter in a saucepan, add the mushrooms and sweat gently for 2 minutes. Pour in the wine and reduce by one-third, then add the fish stock and bring to the boil. Immediately whisk in the cooled blond roux, a little at a time. Cook the sauce at a very gentle bubble for 30 minutes, whisking it and skimming the surface every 10 minutes.

Add the cream and cook until the sauce will coat the back of a spoon, then whisk in the pistachio butter, a small piece at a time. As soon as it is all incorporated, stop the cooking, season the sauce to taste and pass it through a fine-mesh conical sieve. Serve it within a few minutes, or keep it warm in a bain-marie, but do not allow it to boil.

SWEAT THE MUSHROOMS IN THE MELTED BUTTER

WHISK IN THE ROUX AND BUBBLE THE SAUCE FOR 30 MINUTES

ADD THE CREAM AND COOK UNTIL THE SAUCE WILL COAT THE BACK OF A SPOON

WHISK IN THE PISTACHIO BUTTER

Matelote Sauce

Sauce matelote

Matelote sauce is customarily served with baby onions and tiny button mushroom caps cooked in butter. It goes very well with whole pan-fried trout, whiting, monkfish tail and many other fish. I sometimes finish the sauce with 100g langoustine butter (page 57), which replaces the 50g chilled butter. This makes it very delicate and perfect for serving with sea bass.

Serves 4
PREPARATION TIME: 5 MINUTES
COOKING TIME: ABOUT 20 MINUTES

Ingredients:
250ML FISH STOCK (PAGE 21)
50G BUTTON MUSHROOMS, THINLY SLICED
400ML FISH VELOUTÉ (PAGE 21)
50G BUTTER, CHILLED AND DICED
SALT AND CAYENNE PEPPER

Put the fish stock and mushrooms in a saucepan and cook over medium heat until half the liquid has evaporated. Add the fish *velouté* and bubble the sauce gently for 10 minutes, then pass it through a wire-mesh conical sieve into a clean pan. Off the heat, whisk in the butter, a little at a time. Season the sauce to taste with salt and cayenne pepper.

RED MATELOTE SAUCE: For a red matelote, use fish stock made with red wine and substitute veal stock (page 16) for the fish *velouté* to give the sauce a deep amber colour.

PAN-FRIED SEA BASS ON
SAUTERNES SAUCE WITH
PISTACHIOS

Normandy Sauce

Sauce normande

*This classic sauce is wonderful not only with sole à la
normande, but with any white fish. The addition of mussel
juices makes it even more delicious.*

Serves 6
PREPARATION TIME: 15 MINUTES
COOKING TIME: ABOUT 35 MINUTES

Ingredients:
30G BUTTER
100G BUTTON MUSHROOMS, THINLY SLICED
1 SPRIG OF THYME
60G WHITE ROUX, HOT (PAGE 33)
500ML FISH STOCK, COOLED (PAGE 21)
50ML MUSSEL JUICES (OPTIONAL)
200ML DOUBLE CREAM, MIXED WITH 3 EGG YOLKS
JUICE OF 1/2 LEMON
SALT AND FRESHLY GROUND WHITE PEPPER

In a saucepan, melt the butter over low heat, add the
mushrooms and thyme and sweat them for 2 minutes.
Stir in the hot white roux, then pour in the cold fish
stock and mussel juices, if you are using them. Mix
with a small whisk and bring to the boil. Bubble the
sauce gently for 20 minutes, stirring it with the whisk
every 5 minutes. Add the cream and egg yolk mixture
and the lemon juice and continue to bubble the sauce
gently for another 10 minutes. Season to taste with salt
and white pepper, pass the sauce through a wire-mesh
conical sieve and serve immediately.

Seaspray Sauce

Sauce iodée

*This sauce has the tang of the sea. It is excellent served with
braised fish, such as turbot or halibut, or with a fish pie.*

Serves 6
PREPARATION TIME: 5 MINUTES
COOKING TIME: ABOUT 25 MINUTES

Ingredients:
20G BUTTER
40G SHALLOT, CHOPPED
200ML FISH STOCK (PAGE 21)
150ML DRY WHITE WINE
20G MIXED DRIED AROMATICS, GROUND OR
PULVERIZED, CONSISTING OF EQUAL QUANTITIES OF:
LAVENDER FLOWERS, DILL SEEDS, LIME FLOWERS,
JUNIPER BERRIES, CORIANDER SEEDS, RED PIMENTO,
LEMON GRASS
6 SHEETS OF DRIED EDIBLE SEAWEED
200ML DOUBLE CREAM
6 MEDIUM OYSTERS, SHELLED, WITH THEIR JUICES
SALT AND FRESHLY GROUND PEPPER

In a saucepan, melt the butter, add the shallot and
sweat it gently for 1 minute. Pour in the fish stock and
wine, then add the mixed aromatics and seaweed and
cook over medium heat until the liquid has reduced by
half. Add the cream together with the oysters and their
juices and bubble the sauce for 5 minutes.

Transfer the contents of the saucepan to a blender
and whizz for 1 minute. Pass the sauce through a wire-
mesh conical sieve into a small saucepan and stand it in
a bain-marie. Season to taste with salt and pepper and
serve immediately, or keep the sauce warm in the
bain-marie for a few minutes.

Raspberry-scented Oyster Sauce

Sauce aux huitres au parfum de framboises

OYSTERS IN A PUFF PASTRY CASE
WITH RASPBERRY-SCENTED
OYSTER SAUCE

A sauce which subtly combines the flavours of raspberries and oysters. I poach raw oysters for just 30 seconds and serve them barely warm in a little dish with this sauce and a scattering of blanched beansprouts... Quite simply sublime!

Serves 6
PREPARATION TIME: 5 MINUTES
COOKING TIME: ABOUT 12 MINUTES

Ingredients:
30G SHALLOT, CHOPPED
18 VERY RIPE RASPBERRIES
20G CASTER SUGAR
50ML RASPBERRY VINEGAR, HOME-MADE (PAGE 44)
OR BOUGHT
8 MEDIUM OYSTERS, SHELLED, WITH THEIR JUICES
200ML DOUBLE CREAM
SALT AND FRESHLY GROUND PEPPER

Combine the shallot, raspberries and sugar in a small saucepan. Cook gently for 3–4 minutes, stirring with a wooden spoon, until you have an almost jam-like purée. Add the vinegar, bubble for 3 minutes, then add the oysters and cream and simmer gently for 5 minutes. Pour the sauce into a blender and purée for 30 seconds, then pass it through a wire-mesh conical sieve into a clean saucepan. Season to taste and serve the sauce immediately, or keep it warm for a few minutes.

The sauces in this chapter are refined, delicate and unctuous, but above all, light and airy. My favourite is hollandaise, which is glorious served warm with poached, steamed or grilled fish, or with fresh asparagus. Numerous other sauces derive from this wonderful, eggy emulsified creation.

Mayonnaise also forms the basis of many derivatives. It can be lightened with whipped cream, yoghurt or, if you want to reduce the calorie count, fromage blanc.

Emulsion Sauces

Also included in this chapter are whisked emulsion sauces like beurre blanc, which should be made with a really good quality dry white wine. This can be replaced by dry sherry if the sauce is to be served with braised white fish like turbot.

All these sauces are simple and quick to make. You must, however, observe a few basic rules.

* Always use a thick-bottomed stainless steel or copper saucepan with straight or sloping sides.
* Hot emulsion sauces are delicate and ethereal. They cannot be kept waiting, so must be prepared just before serving. As their cooking temperature of not more than 65°C makes them an ideal breeding ground for bacteria, they should be served immediately.
* Many emulsion sauces are prepared with raw or lightly cooked eggs. In view of government concerns over the safety of eggs, I would recommend that you use pasteurized eggs where appropriate, although if you can only find these in dried form, they are obviously not suitable for sauces such as mayonnaise. If you do use fresh eggs, make sure that they come from a reliable source and do not serve them raw to people who may be particularly at risk, such as the elderly or very young.
* Hot emulsion sauces should not be reheated, even in a bain-marie. They will lose their lightness and may split.
* Always serve emulsion sauces in a porcelain or stainless steel sauceboat, never silver, as they will tarnish the metal and can rapidly oxidize.

CAULIFLOWER WITH
RED PEPPER SABAYON

Mayonnaise

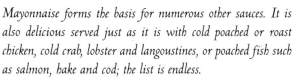

Sauce mayonnaise

ABOVE AND BELOW: WHISK
UNTIL THE MAYONNAISE
BECOMES THICK AND GLOSSY

Mayonnaise forms the basis for numerous other sauces. It is also delicious served just as it is with cold poached or roast chicken, cold crab, lobster and langoustines, or poached fish such as salmon, hake and cod; the list is endless.

If you prefer, you can replace some of the groundnut oil with olive oil, but do not use more than one-quarter, as olive oil has a very pronounced flavour. For a creamier mayonnaise, mix in 2 tablespoons double cream after adding the warm vinegar or cold lemon juice.

Serves 4
PREPARATION TIME: 5 MINUTES

Ingredients:
2 EGG YOLKS
1 TBSP STRONG DIJON MUSTARD
250ML GROUNDNUT OIL
1 TBSP WHITE WINE VINEGAR, WARMED, OR
1 TBSP COLD LEMON JUICE
SALT AND FRESHLY GROUND PEPPER

Lay a tea towel on the work surface and stand a mixing or salad bowl on the towel. In the bowl, combine the egg yolks, mustard and a little salt and pepper (1) and mix with a whisk (2). Pour in the oil in a thin, steady stream, whisking continuously (3). When it is all incorporated, whisk more vigorously for 30 seconds to make a thick, glossy mayonnaise, then add the hot vinegar or cold lemon juice (4). Adjust the seasoning with salt and pepper.

The mayonnaise can be kept at room temperature, covered with cling film, until ready to use. However, it is not wise to keep it for more than a few hours unless you use pasteurized eggs.

MAYONNAISE MAKES A
WONDERFUL DIP FOR
CRUSTACEANS

Aïoli

L'aïoli

This sauce is excellent with salt cod, bouillabaisse (it is much better than the traditional rouille), fish soups and innumerable Mediterranean vegetables. Potatoes do not figure in a classic aïoli, but I like the rustic, creamy quality they add to the sauce.

Serves 8
PREPARATION TIME: 15 MINUTES

Ingredients:
180G BAKED POTATO PULP, RUBBED THROUGH A
SIEVE AND KEPT AT ROOM TEMPERATURE
4 GARLIC CLOVES, PEELED, GREEN SHOOT
REMOVED, AND CRUSHED (PAGE 8)
1 RAW EGG YOLK
2 HARD-BOILED EGG YOLKS, RUBBED THROUGH
A SIEVE
200ML OLIVE OIL
A PINCH OF SAFFRON THREADS, INFUSED IN 3 TBSP
BOILING WATER
SALT AND CAYENNE PEPPER

In a mortar, combine the potato pulp, garlic, raw and cooked egg yolks and a pinch of salt if you wish. Crush these ingredients with a pestle until well amalgamated, then start to trickle in the olive oil in a thin, steady stream, working the mixture continuously with the pestle. When about half the oil has been incorporated, add the saffron and the hot infusion, still mixing as you go. Trickle in the remaining oil, working it in with the pestle to make a smooth, homogeneous sauce. Season with a good pinch of cayenne and salt to taste.

Rémoulade Sauce

Sauce rémoulade

This piquant sauce is perfect for a cold buffet, with assorted cold meats or as a condiment for picnic food like pressed tongue and roast pork or chicken.

Serves 6
PREPARATION TIME: 3 MINUTES

Ingredients:
1 QUANTITY MAYONNAISE (PAGE 109)
40G CORNICHONS OR GHERKINS, FINELY CHOPPED
20G CAPERS, FINELY CHOPPED
1 TBSP SNIPPED FLAT-LEAF PARSLEY
1 TBSP SNIPPED CHERVIL
1 TBSP SNIPPED TARRAGON
1 ANCHOVY FILLET, CRUSHED WITH THE FLAT OF A
CHEF'S KNIFE AND FINELY CHOPPED
1 TSP DIJON MUSTARD, CHILLED
SALT AND FRESHLY GROUND PEPPER

Put the mayonnaise in a bowl and mix in all the other ingredients with a spatula. Season to taste.

Sea Urchin Sauce

Sauce aux oursins

Accentuate the flavour of cold crustaceans such as lobster, crab, spider crab or langoustines with this delicate sea urchin sauce.

Serves 4
PREPARATION TIME: 5 MINUTES

Ingredients:
CORALS OF 12 SEA URCHINS (CUT THEM
OPEN WITH SCISSOR TIPS AND SCRAPE OUT THE
CORALS WITH A TEASPOON)
1 QUANTITY MAYONNAISE (PAGE 109)
1 TBSP MANDARINE NAPOLEON LIQUEUR
OR GRAND MARNIER
100ML WHIPPING CREAM, WHIPPED TO A RIBBON
CONSISTENCY
6 DROPS OF TABASCO
SALT

Rub the sea urchin corals through a fine sieve, then fold them into the mayonnaise with a whisk. Delicately fold in the other ingredients with a spatula and season the sauce with salt.

Gribiche Sauce

Sauce gribiche

Gribiche sauce was one of those that I most often concocted during the 1960s when I was chef to Mlle Cécile de Rothschild. She requested this sauce incessantly; she adored it served with cold fish, crustaceans, shellfish, smoked trout and hard-boiled eggs — in fact, with almost everything.

Serves 6
PREPARATION TIME: 5 MINUTES

Ingredients:
4 FRESHLY COOKED HARD-BOILED EGG YOLKS
1 TSP STRONG DIJON MUSTARD
250ML GROUNDNUT OIL
1 TBSP WHITE WINE VINEGAR
WHITES OF 2 OF THE HARD-BOILED EGGS,
COARSELY CHOPPED
30G SMALL CAPERS, DRAINED, AND
CHOPPED IF THEY ARE LARGE
30G CORNICHONS, FINELY DICED
2 TBSP FINES HERBES (PAGE 10), FINELY SNIPPED
SALT AND FRESHLY GROUND PEPPER

Put the egg yolks, mustard and a little salt and pepper in a mortar and crush with the pestle to make a smooth paste. Gradually trickle in half the oil, mixing with the pestle as you go to amalgamate it thoroughly. Still mixing, add the vinegar, then continue to trickle in the remaining oil in the same way as before. Finally, add all the other ingredients, mix them in with a spoon and season the sauce to taste with salt and pepper.

Swedish Sauce

Sauce suédoise

This sauce makes a good accompaniment to cold roast goose or pork, or to any thinly sliced cold smoked meats.

Serves 6
PREPARATION TIME: 10 MINUTES
COOKING TIME: ABOUT 20 MINUTES

Ingredients:
200G TART DESSERT APPLES, PEELED, CORED AND
CUT INTO CHUNKS
50ML DRY WHITE WINE
1 QUANTITY MAYONNAISE (PAGE 109)
1 TBSP FRESHLY GRATED HORSERADISH
SALT AND FRESHLY GROUND PEPPER

Put the apples and white wine in a saucepan, cover and cook over low heat for 15–20 minutes, until the apples are soft enough to be crushed with a fork. Turn off the heat and rub the apples through a sieve into a bowl. Reserve them in a cool place.

As soon as the apples are cold, mix them into the mayonnaise together with the horseradish, then season the sauce with salt and pepper.

Low Calorie Mayonnaise

Sauce mayonnaise diététique

This low fat mayonnaise can be used to accompany the same dishes as classic mayonnaise. It is refreshing and full of flavour and because it is very low in calories, it is ideal for those on a diet. If you wish, add some snipped chives, mint, tarragon or chervil to the mayonnaise just before serving.

Serves 4
PREPARATION TIME: 3 MINUTES

Ingredients:
150G FROMAGE FRAIS (WHICHEVER FAT
CONTENT YOU PREFER)
1 EGG YOLK
1 TSP STRONG DIJON MUSTARD
1 TSP WHITE WINE VINEGAR OR LEMON JUICE
SALT AND FRESHLY GROUND PEPPER

Place all the ingredients in a mixing or salad bowl and whisk until completely homogeneous. Adjust the seasoning and serve.

PURÉE THE CHLOROPHYLL
INGREDIENTS IN A BLENDER

POUR THE PURÉE ON TO
THE MUSLIN

FOLD UP THE EDGES OF
THE MUSLIN AND TWIST
GENTLY

Green Sauce

Sauce verte

This mayonnaise-based green sauce is wonderful served with cold fish, including smoked trout and eel. The chlorophyll can be used in many other hot or cold sauces and adds a unique herby flavour.

Serves 4 (makes 100g chlorophyll)
PREPARATION TIME: 40 MINUTES
COOKING TIME: ABOUT 20 MINUTES

Special equipment:
A LARGE SQUARE OF BUTTER MUSLIN

Ingredients:
I QUANTITY MAYONNAISE (PAGE 109)
I TBSP GROUNDNUT OIL
FINE SALT

For the chlorophyll:
250G LEAF SPINACH, WASHED AND STALKS REMOVED
10G CHERVIL, WASHED AND STALKS REMOVED
30G PARSLEY, WASHED AND STALKS REMOVED
15G TARRAGON, WASHED AND STALKS REMOVED
15G CHIVES
15G SHALLOT, PEELED AND THINLY SLICED
500ML WATER

First make the chlorophyll; you will need to do this in two batches. Put half the ingredients in a blender and whizz first at low speed for I minute, then for another 4 minutes at medium speed. Scrape the resulting herb purée into a bowl and repeat the process.

Stretch the muslin loosely over a saucepan and secure it with string to stop it slipping. Pour the herb purée into the muslin and leave the liquid to filter through. When most of it has dripped into the pan, remove the string, fold up the edges of the muslin and twist gently to extract as much liquid as possible. Discard the herb purée and rinse the muslin in cold water.

Set the pan containing the bright green juice over low heat and bring to a simmer, stirring occasionally with a wooden spoon. Add a pinch of salt and, as soon as the liquid begins to tremble, turn off the heat.

POUR THE CHLOROPHYLL
ON TO THE MUSLIN AND
DRAIN WELL

SCRAPE OFF THE
CHLOROPHYLL WITH A
PALETTE KNIFE

COVER THE CHLOROPHYLL
WITH A FILM OF OIL

ADD AS MUCH CHLOROPHYLL AS
YOU WISH TO THE MAYONNAISE

MIX THE TWO SAUCES TOGETHER
WITH A WHISK

Stretch the muslin very loosely over a bowl and secure it with string as before, then delicately ladle the contents of the saucepan on to the muslin. Leave for a few minutes to drain well, then use a palette knife or spoon to scrape off the soft green purée (chlorophyll) from the surface of the muslin. Place this in a ramekin, pour a trickle of groundnut oil over the surface of the chlorophyll and keep in a cool place until ready to use (it will keep in the fridge for several days).

To make the green sauce, use a whisk to stir as much of the chlorophyll as you wish into the mayonnaise. The quantity will depend on your taste and how much herb flavour you desire.

Vincent Sauce

Sauce Vincent

This sauce, which dates from the 18th century, remains very popular. It is perfect for a summer buffet and is often served with poached salmon, hake or turbot in aspic or a chaud-froid.

Serves 6
PREPARATION TIME: 5 MINUTES

Ingredients:
$^1/_2$ QUANTITY GREEN SAUCE (OPPOSITE)
$^1/_2$ QUANTITY TARTARE SAUCE (PAGE 114)

Mix the two sauces together with a whisk.

Tartare Sauce

Sauce tartare

Tartare sauce is a classic, which is used mainly to accompany any cold cooked fish.

Serves 6
PREPARATION TIME: 5 MINUTES

Ingredients:
3 HARD-BOILED EGG YOLKS, AT ROOM TEMPERATURE
200ML GROUNDNUT OIL
1 TBSP WINE VINEGAR OR LEMON JUICE
20G ONION, FINELY CHOPPED, BLANCHED,
REFRESHED AND WELL DRAINED
3 TBSP MAYONNAISE (PAGE 109)
1 TBSP SNIPPED CHIVES
SALT AND FRESHLY GROUND PEPPER

Put the egg yolks in a mortar and pound with the pestle to make a smooth paste. Season with salt and pepper, then incorporate the oil in a thin stream, stirring continuously with the pestle. When it is all incorporated, add the vinegar or lemon juice, then the onion, chives and mayonnaise and season to taste.

POUND THE EGG YOLKS TO A PASTE IN A MORTAR

ABOVE AND RIGHT: ADD THE OIL IN A THIN STREAM, STIRRING WITH THE PESTLE UNTIL WELL AMALGAMATED

ADD THE ONION AND CHIVES

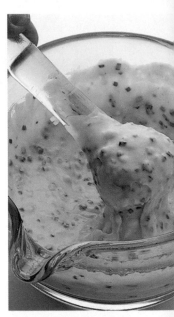

STIR IN THE MAYONNAISE

Alicante Sauce

Sauce Alicante

This is a cold sister sauce to Maltaise sauce (page 119), which is based on a warm hollandaise. Alicante sauce is perfect with cold asparagus, but it should not be chilled before serving. I prefer paprika to cayenne for its colour and flavour, but the choice is yours. As always, once beaten egg whites have been added to the sauce, it cannot be kept waiting.

Serves 6
PREPARATION TIME: 5 MINUTES

Ingredients:
ZEST OF 1 ORANGE, VERY FINELY CHOPPED,
BLANCHED, REFRESHED AND WELL DRAINED
1 QUANTITY MAYONNAISE (PAGE 109), MADE
WITH 1 TBSP LEMON JUICE AND 1 TBSP ORANGE
JUICE (NO VINEGAR)
2 EGG WHITES
SALT AND PAPRIKA OR CAYENNE

Whisk the orange zest into the mayonnaise and add paprika or cayenne, as you prefer. Beat the egg whites stiffly and firm them up with a pinch of salt, then delicately fold them into the mayonnaise. Serve the sauce immediately.

Bagnarotte Sauce

Sauce bagnarotte

This sauce dates back to my days as chef to Mlle Cécile de Rothschild in Paris, and I still often serve it at The Waterside Inn, particularly with canapés in the summer. It is delicious with large pink prawns or crab, ripe cherry tomatoes or raw cauliflower florets. It must be served very cold.

Serves 6
PREPARATION TIME: 3 MINUTES

Ingredients:
1 QUANTITY MAYONNAISE (PAGE 109)
3 TBSP TOMATO KETCHUP
1 TSP WORCESTERSHIRE SAUCE
1 TBSP COGNAC
2 TBSP DOUBLE CREAM
6 DROPS OF TABASCO
JUICE OF 1/2 LEMON
SALT AND FRESHLY GROUND PEPPER

Put the mayonnaise in a bowl and mix in all the other ingredients with a whisk. Season to taste with salt and pepper and keep in the fridge until ready to use.

Alsatian Mustard Sauce with Horseradish

Sauce moutarde au raifort ou alsacienne

I use this sauce in winter to accompany roast or grilled fish. It is also delicious with steamed broccoli or with soft poached eggs served in a ramekin on a bed of sweetcorn sweated in butter.

Serves 6
PREPARATION TIME: 5 MINUTES
COOKING TIME: 12–15 MINUTES

Ingredients:
1 QUANTITY HOLLANDAISE SAUCE (PAGE 116)
1 TBSP ENGLISH MUSTARD POWDER, DISSOLVED IN
1 TBSP COLD WATER
1 TBSP GRATED HORSERADISH
SALT AND FRESHLY GROUND WHITE PEPPER

Just before serving the sauce, whisk in the lemon juice specified in the hollandaise recipe, the mustard and horseradish. Season to taste with salt and pepper and serve immediately.

Hollandaise Sauce

Sauce hollandaise

Hollandaise sauce is one of the great classics and many other sauces derive from it. It is light, smooth and delicate and does not like to be kept waiting; if you cannot serve it immediately, keep it covered in a warm place.

Serves 6 (makes about 700 ml)

PREPARATION TIME: 20 MINUTES
COOKING TIME: 12–15 MINUTES

Ingredients:
4 TBSP COLD WATER
1 TBSP WHITE WINE VINEGAR
1 TSP WHITE PEPPERCORNS, CRUSHED
4 EGG YOLKS
250G BUTTER, FRESHLY CLARIFIED (PAGE 31) AND COOLED TO TEPID
JUICE OF $^1/_2$ LEMON
SALT

THE LEMON JUICE SHOULD BE STIRRED INTO THE HOLLANDAISE SAUCE JUST BEFORE SERVING

Combine the water, vinegar and pepper in a small, heavy-based stainless steel saucepan (1). Over low heat, reduce by one-third, then leave to cool in a cold place.

When the liquid is cold, add the egg yolks (2) and mix thoroughly with a small whisk. Set the saucepan over a very gentle heat and whisk continuously, making sure that the whisk comes into contact with the entire bottom surface of the pan (3). Keep whisking as you gently and progressively increase the heat source; the sauce should emulsify very gradually, becoming smooth and creamy after 8–10 minutes. Do not allow the temperature of the sauce to rise above 65°C.

Take the saucepan off the heat and, whisking continuously, blend in the cooled clarified butter, a little at a time (4). Season the sauce with salt to taste.

Pass the sauce through a fine-mesh conical sieve and serve as soon as possible, stirring in the lemon juice at the last moment.

NOISETTE SAUCE: 50g *beurre noisette* (browned butter) added just before serving gives hollandaise sauce a delicious flavour and transforms it into a *sauce noisette*.

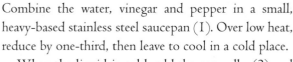

Hollandaise Sauce with Red Butter

Sauce hollandaise au beurre rouge

I like to serve this glorious sauce with grilled lobster or a piece of pan-fried cod garnished with langoustine tails and braised oyster mushrooms.

Serves 6
PREPARATION TIME: 5 MINUTES
COOKING TIME: 12–15 MINUTES

Ingredients:
I QUANTITY HOLLANDAISE SAUCE (PAGE II6), MADE
WITH ONLY I50G CLARIFIED BUTTER
200G LANGOUSTINE BUTTER (PAGE 57)
5G FRESH GINGER, FINELY GRATED
50ML WHIPPING CREAM, WHIPPED TO A FLOPPY
CONSISTENCY WITH THE JUICE OF ½ LEMON
SALT AND FRESHLY GROUND PEPPER

Follow the recipe for hollandaise sauce, gradually whisking in the 150g clarified butter and the shrimp or langoustine butter. Add the lemon juice specified in the recipe and the ginger. Very gently fold in the lemony cream, season with salt and pepper and serve immediately.

Hollandaise Sauce with Fish Stock

Sauce hollandaise au fumet de poisson

This sauce is delicious with pan-fried or grilled turbot or halibut. I sometimes add a few spoons of the cooking juices from shellfish to the fish stock before reducing it, which further enhances the sauce.

Serves 6
PREPARATION TIME: 5 MINUTES
COOKING TIME: ABOUT 20 MINUTES

Ingredients:
I00ML FISH STOCK (PAGE 21)
I QUANTITY HOLLANDAISE SAUCE (PAGE II6)
I TBSP SNIPPED DILL
50G WHIPPING CREAM, WHIPPED TO SOFT PEAKS
SALT AND FRESHLY GROUND PEPPER

Pour the fish stock into a small saucepan and reduce over low heat to only 2 tablespoons. Whisk this reduction into the hollandaise sauce, then add the lemon juice specified in the recipe, the dill and the cream. Season to taste and serve at once.

Mousseline Sauce

Sauce mousseline

This delicate sauce is perfect for serving with poached or steamed fish or with asparagus. When truffles are in season, I add some chopped truffle trimmings, which make the sauce even more delectable.

Ingredients:
1 QUANTITY HOLLANDAISE SAUCE (PAGE 116)
75ML WHIPPING CREAM, WHIPPED TO SOFT PEAKS
SALT AND FRESHLY GROUND PEPPER

Just before serving the sauce, whisk the lemon juice specified in the recipe and the whipped cream into the hollandaise. Season and serve immediately.

Maltaise Sauce

Sauce maltaise

I like to serve this with crisply cooked mange-tout mixed with some orange segments and asparagus. It also goes very well with poached salmon trout.

Serves 6
PREPARATION TIME: 5 MINUTES
COOKING TIME: 12–15 MINUTES

Ingredients:
JUICE OF 1 LARGE BLOOD ORANGE (PREFERABLY),
OR OF 2 SMALL ORANGES
ZEST FROM THE ORANGE, VERY FINELY CHOPPED,
BLANCHED, REFRESHED AND WELL DRAINED
1 QUANTITY HOLLANDAISE SAUCE (PAGE 116)
SALT AND FRESHLY GROUND PEPPER

Put the orange juice in a small saucepan, set over low heat and reduce by one-third, then add the zests and take the pan off the heat. Just before serving, whisk the lemon juice specified in the recipe into the hollandaise sauce, together with the reduced orange juice and zests. Serve immediately.

Beurre Blanc with Cream

Beurre blanc à la crème

Like all beurres blancs, this must be made with the best quality unsalted butter. This delicate sauce is simple to make and is delicious with almost any poached fish.

Serves 6
PREPARATION TIME: 10 MINUTES
COOKING TIME: ABOUT 15 MINUTES

Ingredients:
100ML WHITE WINE VINEGAR
60G SHALLOTS, FINELY CHOPPED
2 TBSP WATER
50ML DOUBLE CREAM
200G BUTTER, CHILLED AND DICED
SALT AND FRESHLY GROUND WHITE PEPPER

Combine the vinegar, shallots and water in a small, thick-bottomed saucepan and reduce the liquid over low heat by two-thirds. Add the cream and reduce again by one-third. Over low heat, whisk in the butter, a little at a time, or beat it in with a wooden spoon. It is vital to keep the sauce barely simmering at 90°C and not to let it boil during this operation. Season with salt and pepper and serve immediately.

BEURRE ROUGE WITH CREAM: You can make a red version of this by substituting an equal quantity of red wine vinegar for the white wine vinegar.

Cider
Beurre Blanc

Beurre blanc au cidre

I adore this butter sauce served with grilled scallops, a simply poached sole on the bone, braised turbot or a John Dory roasted in the oven and served whole at the table.

Serves 6
PREPARATION TIME: 10 MINUTES
COOKING TIME: 15 MINUTES

Ingredients:
80ML CIDER VINEGAR
60G SHALLOTS, FINELY CHOPPED
100ML SWEET CIDER
50G DESSERT APPLE (PREFERABLY COX),
PEELED AND FINELY GRATED
250G BUTTER, CHILLED AND DICED
SALT AND FRESHLY GROUND PEPPER

Put the vinegar and shallot in a small, thick-bottomed saucepan, set over low heat and reduce the liquid by half. Add the cider and grated apple and cook gently to reduce the liquid by one-third. Still over low heat, incorporate the butter, a little at a time, using a whisk or small wooden spoon. The butter sauce must not boil, but merely tremble at about 90°C. Season to taste with salt and pepper and serve immediately, or keep the sauce warm for a few minutes in a bain-marie.

Champagne
Beurre Blanc

Beurre blanc au Champagne

This sauce is wonderful with poached chicken or guinea fowl, and equally good with whole braised fish, such as John Dory or baby turbot.

Serves 6
PREPARATION TIME: 10 MINUTES
COOKING TIME: ABOUT 20 MINUTES

Ingredients:
50ML CHAMPAGNE VINEGAR
60G SHALLOTS, FINELY CHOPPED
1 SPRIG OF THYME
100ML BRUT CHAMPAGNE
60G BUTTON MUSHROOMS, VERY FINELY DICED
250G BUTTER, CHILLED AND DICED
SALT AND FRESHLY GROUND WHITE PEPPER

Combine the vinegar, shallots and thyme in a small, thick-bottomed saucepan and reduce the liquid by half over low heat. Add the Champagne and mushrooms and continue to cook gently until the liquid has again reduced by half. Remove the thyme. Over low heat, whisk in the butter, a little at a time, or beat it in with a wooden spoon. It is vital to keep the sauce barely simmering at 90°C and not to let it boil during this operation. Season to taste and serve the sauce at once, or keep it hot in a bain-marie for a few minutes.

CIDER BEURRE BLANC
WITH SCALLOPS

ADD THE CHOPPED PEPPER TO
THE SAUCEPAN

SIMMER FOR 15 MINUTES
THEN WHISK THE EGG YOLKS
INTO THE ALMOST COLD
SAUCE

Red Pepper Sabayon

Sabayon au poivron rouge

I serve this sabayon with poached eggs on a bed of pilaff rice, or with vegetables like cauliflower and asparagus. It is also good with grilled fish, particularly salmon escalopes.

The vegetable stock can be replaced by chicken or fish stock, depending on the dish the sauce is to accompany.

Serves 4
PREPARATION TIME: 10 MINUTES
COOKING TIME: ABOUT 25 MINUTES

Ingredients:
200G RED PEPPER
200ML VEGETABLE STOCK (PAGE 22)
1 SMALL SPRIG OF THYME
4 EGG YOLKS
60G BUTTER, CHILLED AND DICED
SALT AND FRESHLY GROUND PEPPER

Halve the red pepper lengthways and remove the stalk, seeds and white membranes. Coarsely chop the pepper, place it in a small saucepan with the stock and thyme and simmer for 15 minutes. Pour the contents of the saucepan into a blender and whizz for 1 minute. Pass the purée through a wire-mesh conical sieve into a small clean saucepan and leave until almost cold, then whisk in the egg yolks. Stand the pan in a bain-marie or over indirect heat and whisk the *sabayon* to a ribbon consistency. Whisk in the butter, a little at a time, season the *sabayon* with salt and pepper and serve at once.

RIGHT: HALVE THE
PEPPER LENGTHWAYS

WHISK TO A RIBBON
CONSISTENCY

WHISK THE BUTTER IN
THE SABAYON

Béarnaise Sauce

Sauce béarnaise

This sauce is wonderful with grilled steak and beef fondue. I eat it just on its own, spread on a piece of bread.

Serves 6
PREPARATION TIME: 20 MINUTES
COOKING TIME: 12–15 MINUTES

Ingredients:
2 TBSP WHITE WINE VINEGAR
3 TBSP SNIPPED TARRAGON
30G SHALLOT, FINELY CHOPPED
10 PEPPERCORNS, CRUSHED
4 EGG YOLKS
3 TBSP COLD WATER
250G FRESHLY CLARIFIED BUTTER (PAGE 31),
COOLED TO TEPID
2 TBSP SNIPPED CHERVIL
JUICE OF $1/2$ LEMON
SALT AND FRESHLY GROUND PEPPER

Combine the vinegar, 2 tbsp tarragon, the shallot and peppercorns in a small, thick-bottomed saucepan, and reduce by half over low heat. Set aside in a cool place.

When the vinegar reduction is cold, add the egg yolks and cold water. Set the pan over low heat and whisk continuously, making sure that the whisk reaches right down into the bottom of the pan. As you whisk, gently increase the heat; the sauce should emulsify slowly and gradually, becoming unctuous after 8–10 minutes. Do not let it become hotter than 65°C.

Turn off the heat and whisk the clarified butter into the sauce, a little at a time. Season with salt and pepper and pass the sauce through a wire-mesh conical sieve into another pan. Stir in the rest of the tarragon, the chervil and lemon juice and serve at once.

CHORON SAUCE: 2 tablespoons well-reduced cooked tomato coulis (page 66) added to the béarnaise will give you a Choron sauce.

FOYOT SAUCE: Add 2 tablespoons veal *demi-glace* (page 16) to the béarnaise to make a Foyot sauce.

Paloise Sauce

Sauce paloise

This is basically a béarnaise sauce flavoured with mint instead of tarragon. It is excellent with roast or grilled lamb, and often appears on the menu at The Waterside Inn.

Serves 6
PREPARATION TIME: 20 MINUTES
COOKING TIME: 12–15 MINUTES

Ingredients:
1 QUANTITY BÉARNAISE SAUCE (LEFT), MADE
WITHOUT TARRAGON
1 TBSP SNIPPED MINT LEAVES

Follow the recipe for béarnaise sauce, substituting two-thirds of the mint for the tarragon. Pass the sauce through a wire-mesh conical sieve, then add the lemon juice, chervil and the remaining mint. Serve immediately.

GRILLED LAMB CUTLETS
WITH PALOISE SAUCE

CHAPTER 8

The ivory paleness, creamy whiteness or delicate blond colouring of these sauces makes them appealing and easy on the eye. Their main components are white chicken or lamb stock (made without colouring the bones or carcasses), or milk, often with the addition of some cream.

White Sauces

They are usually thickened with a white or blond roux or egg yolks, or they may be bound or smoothed with butter. Herbs, spices, relishes, white wine or sherry add an extra dimension and individuality.

The best way to eat these light, adaptable sauces is with a spoon. They are at their most appealing in the winter, served with poached or boiled poultry, white meats, offal and certain fish.

The king of the white sauces is béchamel, from which many other sauces derive, each as delicious as the last. Through the centuries, béchamel has continued to top the hit parade of our culinary heritage.

MACARONI AU GRATIN MADE
WITH A BÉCHAMEL SAUCE

Béchamel Sauce

Sauce béchamel

This is the ideal sauce for any number of dishes, such as cauliflower or endive au gratin, *macaroni cheese made with a touch of cream and grated gruyère or emmenthal, a genuine croque monsieur — the list is endless. Like hollandaise, mayonnaise and crème anglaise, béchamel forms the basis of innumerable other sauces.*

STIR THE BÉCHAMEL CONTINUOUSLY WHILE COOKING

Serves 4
PREPARATION TIME: 5 MINUTES
COOKING TIME: ABOUT 25 MINUTES

Ingredients:
500ML MILK
60G WHITE ROUX (PAGE 33), COOLED
FRESHLY GRATED NUTMEG (OPTIONAL)
SALT AND FRESHLY GROUND WHITE PEPPER

PASS THE BÉCHAMEL SAUCE THROUGH A CONICAL STRAINER

Put the cold roux into a small, thick-bottomed saucepan. Bring the milk to the boil and pour it on to the roux, mixing and stirring with a whisk or wooden spatula. Set the pan over low heat and bring the mixture to the boil, still stirring continuously. As soon as it reaches boiling point, reduce the heat and cook at a very gentle simmer for about 20 minutes, stirring the sauce continuously and making sure that the whisk scrapes across all the surfaces of the pan.

SEASON WITH A LITTLE NUTMEG (OPTIONAL)

Season the sauce with salt, white pepper and a very little nutmeg if you wish, then pass it through a conical strainer. You can serve it immediately or keep it warm in a bain-marie, in which case dot a few flakes of butter over the surface to prevent a skin from forming.

Béchamel sauce will keep in an airtight container in the fridge for a maximum of four days.

CLASSIC RICH BÉCHAMEL: The old classic rich béchamel was made with the addition of veal. To make this, sweat 75g diced veal and 30g chopped onion in 30g butter (1). In another pan make a basic béchamel (2 and 3) and when it reaches boiling point, add the veal and onions (4) and continue with the recipe as above.

DOT FLAKES OF BUTTER OVER THE SURFACE TO PREVENT A SKIN FROM FORMING

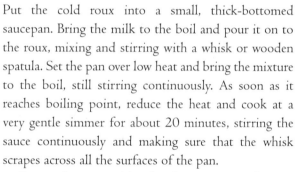

Coconut and Chilli Pepper Sauce

Sauce à la noix de coco et aux piments

Serve this unusual, spicy sauce with wide noodles or any poached firm-fleshed white fish.

Serves 8
PREPARATION TIME: 10 MINUTES
COOKING TIME: 25 MINUTES

Ingredients:
100G BUTTER
10G SMALL HOT RED CHILLIES, DESEEDED AND
FINELY CHOPPED
20G HOT GREEN JALAPENO PEPPERS, DESEEDED AND
FINELY CHOPPED
250G SMALL PEELED SHRIMPS OR
PRAWNS (OPTIONAL)

For the coconut béchamel:
30G BUTTER
30G FLOUR
400ML CANNED COCONUT MILK
FRESHLY GRATED NUTMEG
SALT AND FRESHLY GROUND PEPPER
2 GARLIC CLOVES, CRUSHED OR FINELY CHOPPED
1 TBSP SOY SAUCE

ADD THE CHOPPED CHILLIES TO THE
BROWNED BUTTER

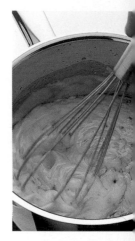

ADD THE MIXTURE TO
THE COCONUT
BÉCHAMEL

First make the coconut béchamel. In a small saucepan, melt the 30g butter and stir in the flour to make a roux. Cook over low heat for 2 minutes, stirring all the time with a whisk. Add the coconut milk, bring to the boil, then immediately season with nutmeg, salt and pepper and cook gently for 20 minutes, stirring continuously. Off the heat, stir in the soy sauce and garlic.

In another small saucepan, heat the 100g butter until it turns fragrant and golden brown. Toss in the chopped chillies and immediately tip the mixture into the coconut béchamel and stir until well amalgamated. Adjust the seasoning if necessary and stir in the shrimps at the last moment, if you are using them. Serve the sauce hot.

STIR UNTIL WELL
AMALGAMATED, THEN
ADD THE SHRIMPS
(OPTIONAL)

Aurora Sauce

Sauce Aurore

Hard-boiled eggs sliced into discs, coated with Aurora sauce and browned under the grill are delicious. The sauce is also very good with poached eggs, pasta, cauliflower or grilled turkey escalopes.

You can substitute a chicken velouté *(page 132) for the béchamel if you prefer the flavour.*

The taste of tomato coulis will vary according to the season; if it is highly scented and coloured, use a little less. If it is pallid and lacking in intensity, use more.

Serves 6
PREPARATION TIME: 5 MINUTES
COOKING TIME: ABOUT 15 MINUTES

Ingredients:
300ML BÉCHAMEL SAUCE (PAGE 128)
100ML DOUBLE CREAM
100ML COOKED TOMATO COULIS (PAGE 66)
20G BUTTER, CHILLED AND DICED
SALT AND FRESHLY GROUND PEPPER OR NUTMEG

Combine the béchamel and cream in a saucepan and bring to the boil over low heat, stirring continuously with a whisk. Bubble the sauce for 5 minutes, then add the tomato coulis, bring the sauce back to the boil and cook for another 5 minutes, whisking continuously. Turn off the heat and whisk in the butter, a little at a time. Season the sauce with salt and pepper or nutmeg, according to taste, pass it through a wire-mesh conical sieve and serve immediately.

Bread Sauce

The perfect sauce to accompany roast chicken or turkey. It is also ideal with roast pheasant or grouse. I often serve it at the restaurant and frequently request it at home.

Serves 4
PREPARATION TIME: 5 MINUTES
COOKING TIME: ABOUT 1 HOUR

Ingredients:
20G BUTTER
60G ONIONS, CHOPPED
400ML MILK
1 WHOLE OR ½ ONION (WEIGHING 60G),
STUDDED WITH 2 CLOVES
80G WHITE BREAD, CRUSTS REMOVED, CUT INTO
CUBES
50ML DOUBLE CREAM
SALT AND FRESHLY GROUND WHITE PEPPER

Melt the butter in a small saucepan, add the chopped onions and sweat them gently for 1 minute. Pour in the milk, add the clove-studded onion and simmer at about 90°C for 20 minutes. Stir in the bread and bring to the boil. Lower the heat and cook the sauce gently for 30 minutes, stirring occasionally with a wooden spoon. Remove the studded onion, add the cream and bubble the sauce gently for 5 minutes, whisking gently. Season with salt and white pepper and serve hot.

Albufera Sauce

Sauce Albufera

This is a sauce for a grand dinner. Poultry, sweetbreads or poached calf's tongue will all benefit from its richness.

Serves 6
PREPARATION TIME: 5 MINUTES

Ingredients:
500ML BOILING CHICKEN VELOUTÉ (PAGE 132)
150ML VEAL DEMI-GLACE (PAGE 16)
50ML FRESH OR PRESERVED TRUFFLE JUICE
(OPTIONAL)
SALT AND CAYENNE PEPPER

Into the boiling chicken *velouté*, whisk the veal *demi-glace* and truffle juice, if using. Season the sauce with salt and cayenne to taste and serve immediately.

Chicken Velouté

Velouté de volaille

This velouté can be used as a base for other sauces; just omit the sherry. Personally, I find it excellent just as it is. I serve it with poached poultry and rice or with a whole pale pan-fried veal sweetbread garnished with leaf spinach.

Serves 6 (makes about 800ml)
PREPARATION TIME: 5 MINUTES
COOKING TIME: ABOUT 30 MINUTES

Ingredients:
60G WHITE ROUX, HOT (PAGE 33)
750ML CHICKEN STOCK, COOLED (PAGE 18)
50ML DRY SHERRY (OPTIONAL)
SALT AND FRESHLY GROUND WHITE PEPPER

Put the hot white roux into a saucepan and add the cold chicken stock. Set over medium heat and bring to the boil, whisking continuously. Reduce the heat and gently simmer the *velouté* for 30 minutes, stirring the sauce and skimming the surface every 10 minutes. Add the sherry if you are using it, and cook for 1 more minute. Season the sauce with salt and white pepper and pass it through a wire-mesh conical sieve.

Sauce Albert

Sauce Albert, which we serve with our pot-au-feu, and cuts like silverside, veal knuckle and beef flank, is one of the legendary Roux brothers' sauces, which our faithful regulars always enjoy. It is also excellent with roast rabbit.

Serves 4
PREPARATION TIME: 15 MINUTES
COOKING TIME: ABOUT 50 MINUTES

Ingredients:
300ML CHICKEN STOCK (PAGE 18),
OR BROTH FROM A POT-AU-FEU
150G HORSERADISH, PREFERABLY FRESHLY GRATED,
OR 200G BOTTLED HORSERADISH, WELL DRAINED
300ML DOUBLE CREAM
50G FRESH WHITE BREAD, CRUSTS REMOVED, CUT
INTO SMALL CUBES
1 EGG YOLK
1 TSP ENGLISH MUSTARD POWDER, DISSOLVED IN
1 TBSP COLD WATER
SALT AND FRESHLY GROUND WHITE PEPPER

Combine the chicken stock or broth and the horseradish in a small saucepan, set over medium heat and boil for 15 minutes. Add the cream and bubble gently for another 20 minutes. Transfer the sauce to a blender and whizz for 1 minute (you may have to do this in two batches), then pass the sauce through a wire-mesh conical sieve into a clean saucepan.

Add the cubes of bread and cook the sauce over low heat for 10 minutes, whisking continuously. Turn off the heat, add the egg yolk and mustard and stir for a few moments before vigorously whisking the sauce to make it very smooth; it should have the consistency of porridge. Season to taste with salt and pepper and serve at once. If you need to keep the sauce warm, do not let it boil.

Mustard and White Wine Sauce

Sauce moutarde au vin blanc

This versatile sauce is perfect served with pot-roasted poultry or white meats. For these, make the sauce with chicken stock, but obviously if you are going to serve it with poached or braised fish (preferably firm-fleshed), use fish stock instead.

Serves 4
PREPARATION TIME: 10 MINUTES
COOKING TIME: ABOUT 40 MINUTES

Ingredients:
30G BUTTER
80G BUTTON MUSHROOMS, THINLY SLICED
60G SHALLOTS, FINELY CHOPPED
A PINCH OF CURRY POWDER
1 TBSP COGNAC OR ARMAGNAC
200ML DRY WHITE WINE
1 SMALL BOUQUET GARNI (PAGE 10)
200ML FISH STOCK (PAGE 21)
OR CHICKEN STOCK (PAGE 18)
300ML DOUBLE CREAM
1 TSP ENGLISH MUSTARD POWDER, DISSOLVED
IN A LITTLE WATER
2 TBSP WHOLEGRAIN MUSTARD
SALT AND FRESHLY GROUND PEPPER

SWEAT THE
MUSHROOMS IN
THE BUTTER

ADD THE COGNAC
AND THE WINE

COOK UNTIL THE SAUCE WILL
COAT THE BACK OF THE SPOON

In a saucepan, melt the butter, add the mushrooms and shallot and sweat for 1 minute. Stir in the curry powder and add the Cognac and wine. Bring to the boil, put in the bouquet garni and reduce the liquid by one-third. Pour in the fish or chicken stock, bubble for 5 minutes, then add the cream and the English mustard and cook until the sauce is thick enough to coat the back of a spoon. Remove the bouquet garni, season to taste with salt and pepper and pass the sauce through a wire-mesh conical strainer. Stir in the wholegrain mustard. The sauce is now ready to serve.

STIR IN THE WHOLEGRAIN
MUSTARD

Parsley Sauce

Sauce au persil

This sauce is simplicity itself and most delicious, especially when it is prepared with the cooking liquid from a boiled ham and served with the ham. It also tastes good with plain boiled Brussels sprouts, carrots or potatoes.

You can enrich the sauce with cream or butter, but I prefer it without. Because it is not rich, it can be eaten with a spoon; this is why I suggest that the recipe serves four people rather than six, as you might expect.

Serves 4
PREPARATION TIME: 5 MINUTES
COOKING TIME: ABOUT 20 MINUTES

Ingredients:
350ML COOKING LIQUID FROM A BOILED HAM,
OR CHICKEN STOCK (PAGE 18)
150ML MILK
40G WHITE ROUX, COOLED (PAGE 33)
2 TBSP CHOPPED PARSLEY
A PINCH OF FRESHLY GRATED NUTMEG
SALT AND FRESHLY GROUND WHITE PEPPER

Bring the cooking liquid or stock and the milk to the boil. Put the cold roux in a saucepan and pour on the hot liquid, whisking as you go. Bring to the boil over low heat, stirring continuously with the whisk as the sauce begins to bubble. Add the parsley and simmer the sauce for 15 minutes, skimming the surface with a spoon if necessary. Season with the nutmeg and salt and pepper to taste and serve piping hot.

Supreme Sauce with Sherry

Sauce suprême au sherry

A classic supreme sauce is made without sherry, but I think it adds a theatrical note which pleases me very much. This wonderfully smooth, creamy sauce is subtle and savoury. Serve it with poached poultry, timbales of mushrooms and sweetbreads, braised lettuce or thin pan-fried veal escalopes. It is essential to use the best quality butter to finish this sauce.

Serves 4
PREPARATION TIME: 5 MINUTES
COOKING TIME: ABOUT 10 MINUTES

Ingredients:
250ML BOILING CHICKEN VELOUTÉ (PAGE 132)
50G BUTTON MUSHROOMS, THINLY SLICED
50ML DOUBLE CREAM
30G BUTTER, CHILLED AND DICED
4 TBSP DRY SHERRY
SALT AND FRESHLY GROUND PEPPER

Pour the boiling chicken *velouté* into a saucepan and add the mushrooms and cream. Simmer over low heat for 10 minutes, stirring occasionally with a wooden spoon. Pass the sauce through a wire-mesh conical sieve into a clean saucepan, turn the heat to low and whisk in the butter, a little at a time. Turn off the heat, stir in the sherry, season the sauce with salt and pepper and serve immediately.

BOILED HAM WITH PARSLEY SAUCE

Caper Sauce
with Anchovies

Sauce aux câpres au parfum d'anchois

A lively, vigorous sauce which cuts the richness of offal such as brains, sweetbreads, tripe or calf's head.

Serves 8
PREPARATION TIME: 5 MINUTES
COOKING TIME: 15 MINUTES

Ingredients:
500ML CHICKEN VELOUTÉ (PAGE 132)
1 BOUQUET GARNI (PAGE 10), INCLUDING
2 SPRIGS OF SAVORY
100ML DRY WHITE WINE
100ML DOUBLE CREAM
60G ANCHOVY BUTTER (PAGE 57)
30G SMALL CAPERS (CHOP THEM IF THEY ARE
LARGE), WELL DRAINED
2 ANCHOVY FILLETS, FINELY DICED
SALT AND CAYENNE PEPPER

In a saucepan, bring the *velouté* to the boil, add the bouquet garni and white wine and cook gently for 10 minutes. Pour in the cream and continue to cook gently for another 5 minutes. The sauce should lightly coat the back of a spoon; if it is not thick enough, increase the heat to as high as possible and reduce it for a few more minutes. Lower the heat to minimum, whisk in the anchovy butter, a little at a time, and pass the sauce through a wire-mesh conical sieve into a clean saucepan. Season with cayenne and a very little salt, stir in the capers and diced anchovies and serve at once.

Champagne
Sauce with Morels

Sauce Champagne aux morilles

This is the Champagne sauce which I serve with poached capon. Try this unctuous sauce for a special occasion.

Serves 8
PREPARATION TIME: 10 MINUTES
COOKING TIME: 45 MINUTES

Ingredients:
75G FRESH MORELS, OR 30G DRIED MORELS SOAKED
IN BOILING WATER FOR 1 HOUR
400ML CHICKEN VELOUTÉ (PAGE 132)
200ML BRUT CHAMPAGNE
200ML DOUBLE CREAM
80G FOIE GRAS BUTTER (PAGE 63)
SALT AND FRESHLY GROUND WHITE PEPPER

First clean the fresh morels. Trim the very bottom of the stalks, halve the mushrooms (or quarter them if they are very large), rinse in cold water to remove all traces of grit and delicately pat dry on a tea towel. If you are using dried morels, drain them from their soaking water and proceed as for fresh morels.

Combine the chicken *velouté* and three-quarters of the Champagne in a saucepan and boil over medium heat for 20 minutes. Put the cream and prepared morels in another saucepan and bring to the boil over medium heat. Cook for 5 minutes, then tip the cream and morel mixture into the pan with the *velouté*. Cook at a bare simmer for 15 minutes, removing any skin from the surface with a spoon if necessary.

Add the remaining Champagne, bubble the sauce for 2 minutes and turn off the heat. Add the foie gras butter, a little at a time, mixing it into the sauce with a wooden spoon. Season with salt and white pepper and serve immediately.

RABBIT WITH SORREL SAUCE

Sorrel Sauce

Sauce à l'oseille

This sauce is one of my mother's favourites. Its hint of acidity and freshness makes it ideal for serving with pan-fried lamb chops or roast saddle of rabbit. A few shredded mint leaves added to the sauce just before serving intensify the taste of the sorrel and make the sauce more rounded.

Serves 6
PREPARATION TIME: 5 MINUTES
COOKING TIME: ABOUT 20 MINUTES

Ingredients:
60G SORREL
30G BUTTER
40G SHALLOT, FINELY CHOPPED
100ML WHITE WINE
200ML VEGETABLE STOCK (PAGE 22)
200ML DOUBLE CREAM
SALT AND FRESHLY GROUND PEPPER

Wash the sorrel and remove the stalks. Pile up several leaves, roll them up like a cigar and shred them finely, repeating until you have shredded all the sorrel. Melt the butter in a deep frying pan, add the shallot and sweat it over low heat for 30 seconds, then put in the sorrel and sweat gently for another minute. Pour in the wine and stock and reduce the liquid by two-thirds. Add the cream and bubble for 2 minutes. The sauce should be thick enough to coat the back of a spoon lightly. Season to taste and serve immediately.

Soubise Sauce

Sauce soubise

Perfect for winter, this sauce goes particularly well with roast rack or loin of veal and with roast chicken or guinea fowl. It can be prepared in advance and reheated in a bain-marie.

Serves 4
PREPARATION TIME: 5 MINUTES
COOKING TIME: 25 MINUTES

Ingredients:
40G BUTTER
200G ONIONS, THINLY SLICED
I QUANTITY BÉCHAMEL SAUCE (PAGE 128)
150ML DOUBLE CREAM
FRESHLY GRATED NUTMEG
SALT AND FRESHLY GROUND PEPPER

In a saucepan, melt the butter over low heat, add the onions and sweat for 5 minutes without colouring, stirring gently with a wooden spoon. Add the béchamel, bring to the boil over low heat and bubble gently for 10 minutes, still stirring delicately with the wooden spoon.

Pass the sauce through a wire-mesh sieve into a clean saucepan, pressing the onions through with a wooden food pusher or the back of a small ladle. Add the cream and cook gently for 6–8 minutes, stirring continuously, until the sauce thickens to the consistency of porridge. Season to taste with nutmeg, salt and pepper and serve piping hot.

Butter Sauce

Sauce bâtarde

This water-based sauce (literally 'bastard sauce' in French) relies for all its flavour on the liaison mixture and the butter, which must be of excellent quality. Serve it with poached fish and asparagus, or with boiled vegetables when you want to enhance their flavour without drowning it.

Serves 8
PREPARATION TIME: 10 MINUTES
COOKING TIME: ABOUT 2 MINUTES

Ingredients:
50G WHITE ROUX, COOLED (PAGE 33)
500ML BOILING WATER
120G BUTTER, CHILLED AND DICED
SALT AND A PINCH OF CAYENNE PEPPER

For the liaison:
3 EGG YOLKS MIXED WITH THE JUICE
OF ¹/₂ LEMON AND 2 TBSP DOUBLE CREAM

Put the cold white roux in a saucepan, pour on the boiling water and whisk thoroughly. Set over high heat and bring to the boil, whisking continuously. Boil for 2 or 3 minutes, then turn off the heat and whisk in the liaison mixture. Pass the sauce through a wire-mesh conical sieve into a clean saucepan and whisk in the chilled butter, a little at a time. Season the sauce with salt and cayenne pepper and serve at once.

Mornay Sauce

Sauce Mornay

You can coat a multitude of dishes with this sauce and immediately lightly brown them under a hot grill or salamander; poached eggs, fish, vegetables, white meats are all excellent served this way. Mixed with macaroni, mornay sauce also makes a delicious macaroni cheese.

Serves 4
PREPARATION TIME: 5 MINUTES
COOKING TIME: ABOUT 2 MINUTES

Ingredients:
I QUANTITY BOILING BÉCHAMEL SAUCE (PAGE 128)
50ML DOUBLE CREAM MIXED WITH 3 EGG YOLKS
100G EMMENTHAL, GRUYÈRE OR FARMHOUSE
CHEDDAR, FINELY GRATED
SALT AND FRESHLY GROUND PEPPER

Add the cream and egg yolk mixture to the boiling béchamel and bubble for 1 minute, whisking vigorously. Turn off the heat and mix in your chosen cheese with a wooden spoon. Season the sauce with salt and pepper and use it as you wish.

White Bordelaise or Bonnefoy Sauce

Sauce bordelaise blanche ou Bonnefoy

This robust, well-structured sauce makes the perfect accompaniment to fish with a rather bland flavour, such as whiting, lemon sole, farmed trout or huss.

Serves 4
PREPARATION TIME: 5 MINUTES
COOKING TIME: ABOUT 30 MINUTES

Ingredients:
300ML DRY WHITE WINE
30 ML COGNAC
60G SHALLOTS, FINELY CHOPPED
I BOUQUET GARNI (PAGE 10)
400ML FISH VELOUTÉ (PAGE 21)
40G BUTTER, CHILLED AND DICED
I TBSP SNIPPED TARRAGON LEAVES
SALT AND FRESHLY GROUND PEPPER

Combine the wine, Cognac, shallots and bouquet garni in a saucepan and reduce the liquid to one-third over high heat. Add the fish *velouté* and bubble the sauce gently for 20 minutes, skimming the surface whenever necessary. Pass the sauce through a wire-mesh conical sieve into a clean pan, then whisk in the butter, a little at a time. Season the sauce with salt and pepper, stir in the tarragon and serve at once.

Allemande Sauce

Sauce allemande

This light, silky sauce with its satisfying texture goes very well with poached poultry and offal such as brains and sweetbreads.

Serves 6
PREPARATION TIME: 5 MINUTES
COOKING TIME: 35 MINUTES

Ingredients:
60G SHALLOTS, FINELY CHOPPED
100ML DRY WHITE WINE
10 WHITE PEPPERCORNS, CRUSHED
I BOUQUET GARNI (PAGE 10),
INCLUDING A SPRIG OF SAVORY
500ML CHICKEN STOCK (PAGE 18)
100G BUTTON MUSHROOMS, SLICED
200ML DOUBLE CREAM
SALT AND FRESHLY GROUND WHITE PEPPER

For the liaison:
100ML WHIPPING CREAM, WHIPPED TO
SOFT PEAKS, MIXED WITH 3 EGG YOLKS
AND THE JUICE OF I LEMON

Combine the shallots, white wine, crushed peppercorns and bouquet garni in a saucepan, set over medium heat and reduce the wine by two-thirds. Add the chicken stock and mushrooms and cook until the liquid has reduced by half. Pour in the double cream and bubble the sauce for 5 minutes, or until it lightly coats the back of a spoon.

Pour in the liaison mixture, whisking to amalgamate it thoroughly. Immediately turn off the heat, season the sauce with salt and white pepper, pass it through a wire-mesh conical sieve and at once.

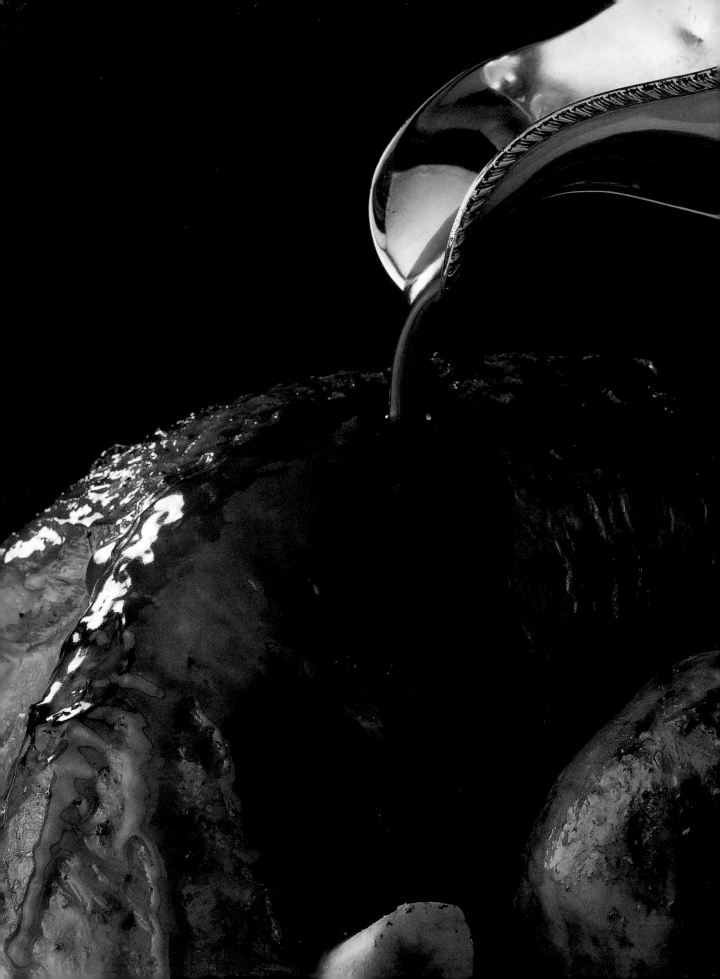

CHAPTER 9

Until the 1960s, the most frequently used and best known brown sauce was espagnole, the ultimate classic sauce which had exemplified French cuisine for generations. It reigned supreme in the kitchens of palaces, hotels and starred restaurants, where it was used as a base or an essential element in any number of sauces, often making them over-rich and heavy.

Brown Sauces

Nowadays, it is really not practical to make this sauce, which is extremely expensive in terms of both ingredients and time; it takes twenty hours or so to complete the two cooking stages — first a brown stock, then the espagnole itself.

I shall always remember the early days of my career, when I was apprenticed to the sauce chef and had to perform the most humble of tasks — the ritual hourly skimming of the stock to ensure that the finished sauce was crystal-clear, with no impurities to impair the flavour. I can see my adolescent face reflected on the surface of the huge stockpot, blurred at first, but becoming clearer and clearer over the hours...

For the past thirty years, veal stock has replaced espagnole sauce in my kitchen. I make it without any thickening agents, so that it is, in fact, a blond veal sauce. It forms the basis of many of my brown sauces, making them velvety, delicate and well-balanced, without masking their vital individuality. When appropriate, I substitute lamb, chicken or duck stock to enhance the flavour of the dish they will accompany.

Brown sauces are among my favourites. They are generally robust, rich and elegant, with a flavour which lingers on the palate. I love their warm, shimmering colours, which range from pale golden to a deep purplish-brown.

ROAST TURKEY
WITH BUCCANEER'S SAUCE

Buccaneer's Sauce

Sauce boucanière

I serve this sauce with veal chops at The Waterside Inn and garnish them with slices of banana pan-fried in butter. You can serve poultry in the same way; the sauce and garnish go well with roast chicken and turkey as well as with roast veal.

Serves 8
PREPARATION TIME: 5 MINUTES
COOKING TIME: ABOUT 25 MINUTES

Ingredients:
40G FRESH GINGER
60G SHALLOTS OR SMALL ONIONS
100G BUTTER
100G BANANA
6 TBSP RASPBERRY VINEGAR, HOME-MADE (PAGE 44)
OR BOUGHT
400ML VEAL STOCK (PAGE 16)
SALT AND FRESHLY GROUND BLACK PEPPER

Peel the ginger with a potato peeler and grate or finely chop it. Peel, wash and thinly slice the shallots or onions. Peel the banana and cut it into rounds.

Melt half the butter in a saucepan, add the chopped shallots or onions and sweat for 1 minute over medium heat. Add the ginger and cook until very lightly coloured, stirring continuously with a spatula. Still stirring, add the banana rounds and cook over low heat for 2 minutes, until the banana softens and begins to disintegrate. Immediately, add the raspberry vinegar and continue to cook over very low heat for another 2 minutes, still stirring.

Add the veal stock and simmer the sauce gently for 20 minutes, then pass it through a conical strainer into another pan. Whisk in the remaining butter, a little at a time, until the sauce is smooth and glossy. Season to taste with salt and pepper.

Light Chicken Gravy with Thyme

Jus de poulet au thym

This is the best possible light gravy to accompany roast poultry. It is also good with fresh pasta, salsify à la meunière, leaf spinach or braised chicory. I adore thyme and, depending on the the intensity of its flavour, which varies according to the season, I may use more or less for this recipe.

Serves 6
PREPARATION TIME: 15 MINUTES
COOKING TIME: 45–60 MINUTES

Ingredients:
3 TBSP GROUNDNUT OIL
1 KG CHICKEN WINGS, COARSELY CHOPPED
100G CARROTS, CHOPPED
100G ONIONS, CHOPPED
200ML DRY WHITE WINE
1 L COLD WATER
5 JUNIPER BERRIES, CRUSHED
1 GARLIC CLOVE, CRUSHED
25G THYME, PREFERABLY FRESH
SALT AND FRESHLY GROUND PEPPER

Heat the oil in a deep frying pan, put in the chicken wings and fry over high heat until golden brown, stirring occasionally with a wooden spoon. Pour off the oil and the fat released by the chicken, then add the carrots and onions. Stir with a wooden spoon and sweat gently for 3 minutes. Pour in the white wine and reduce the liquid by half. Add all the other ingredients, being sparing with the salt and pepper, and bubble the sauce gently for 45 minutes, skimming as often as necessary. Pass it through a conical sieve; it is now ready to serve. For a more concentrated flavour, reduce the sauce over medium heat.

The sauce will keep in an airtight container in the fridge for several days, or for several weeks in the freezer.

Chasseur Sauce

Sauce chasseur

This light savoury sauce is quick to make. It goes very well with poultry and veal.

Serves 8
PREPARATION TIME: 10 MINUTES
COOKING TIME: ABOUT 20 MINUTES

Ingredients:
200G BUTTON MUSHROOMS
100G BUTTER
40G SHALLOT, FINELY CHOPPED
400ML DRY WHITE WINE
400ML VEAL STOCK (PAGE 16)
1 TBSP SNIPPED FLAT-LEAF PARSLEY
1 TSP SNIPPED TARRAGON
SALT AND FRESHLY GROUND BLACK PEPPER

Wipe the mushrooms clean and slice them finely and evenly. Heat half the butter in a shallow pan, add the mushrooms and cook over medium heat for 1 minute. Add the shallot and cook for 1 more minute, taking care not to let it colour.

Tip the mushroom and shallot mixture into a fine-mesh conical sieve to drain off the cooking butter. Put them back into the shallow pan, add the wine and reduce it by half over medium heat. Pour in the veal stock and cook gently for 10–15 minutes, until the sauce is thick enough to coat the back of a spoon.

Take the pan off the heat and whisk in the remaining butter and the snipped herbs. Season to taste with salt and pepper.

CHICKEN WITH CHASSEUR SAUCE

Périgueux Sauce

Sauce Périgueux

This sauce is excellent served with little hot pies or pâtés en croûte, with beef tournedos or pan-fried saddle of lamb, and of course on pasta. To make the sauce richer and more unctuous, whisk in 50g foie gras butter (page 63) just before serving, but omit the 40g chilled butter.

Serves 6
PREPARATION TIME: 5 MINUTES
COOKING TIME: ABOUT 30 MINUTES

Ingredients:
400ML VEAL STOCK (PAGE 16)
50ML BOTTLED TRUFFLE JUICE, OR (PREFERABLY)
THE COOKING JUICE FROM FRESH TRUFFLES
20G TRUFFLES, FINELY CHOPPED
40G BUTTER, WELL-CHILLED AND DICED
SALT AND FRESHLY GROUND PEPPER

In a small saucepan, reduce the veal stock over medium heat (1) until it forms a veil and lightly coats the back of a spoon (2). Add the truffle juice (3) and cook for another 5 minutes. Add the chopped truffles (4) and give the sauce a bubble. Take the pan off the heat and add the butter, one piece at a time, swirling and rotating the pan to incorporate it (5). Season the sauce with salt and pepper to taste and serve immediately (6).

PÉRIGOURDINE SAUCE: You can replace the chopped truffles with truffles sliced into discs or 'turned' into olive shapes. The sauce is then known as *Périgourdine*.

USE THE JUICE FROM FRESHLY-COOKED PRESERVED TRUFFLES

FINELY CHOP THE TRUFFLES

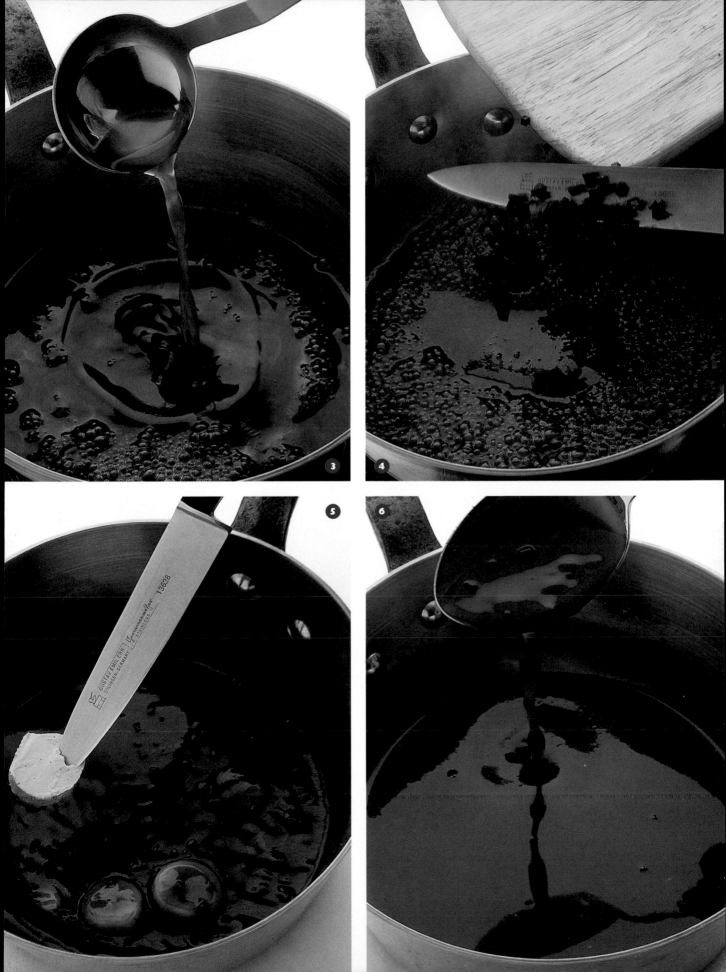

Charcutière Sauce

Sauce charcutière

A memory from my childhood... This homely sauce accompanied the pork chops and mashed potatoes which our grandfather and father served to the customers at their charcuterie in Charolles. If there was any left over, they would serve it to us the next day with a dish of wide noodles.

I prefer this rather piquant sauce to have a slightly thick consistency, which I think complements the texture of pork.

Serves 4
PREPARATION TIME: 5 MINUTES
COOKING TIME: ABOUT 20 MINUTES

Ingredients:
30G BUTTER
60G ONIONS, FINELY CHOPPED
100ML DRY WHITE WINE
300ML VEAL STOCK (PAGE 16)
1 TBSP STRONG DIJON MUSTARD
40G BEURRE MANIÉ (PAGE 31)
30G CORNICHONS, CUT INTO LONG, THIN STRIPS
SALT AND FRESHLY GROUND PEPPER

TO MAKE A BEURRE MANIÉ, MASH BUTTER AND FLOUR WITH A FORK

ADD THE VEAL STOCK

In a small saucepan, melt 30g butter, add the onions and sweat gently without colouring for 1 minute. Pour in the wine and reduce by half over medium heat. Add the veal stock and bubble the sauce gently until it is thick enough to coat the back of a spoon. Whisk in the mustard and the *beurre manié*, a little at a time, and cook for another 2 minutes. Season to taste with salt and pepper. Pass the sauce through a conical sieve into a small saucepan containing the cornichons and serve it immediately, or keep it warm for a few minutes in a bain-marie set over low heat.

POUR THE WINE OVER THE ONIONS

POUR THE SAUCE INTO THE PAN CONTAINING THE CORNICHON STRIPS

WHISK IN THE MUSTARD AND THE BEURRE MANIÉ

Light Lamb Gravy Scented with Lavender Honey

Jus d'agneau au parfum de miel de lavande

This is a lovely sauce to serve with grilled lamb chops or a roast leg of lamb. Or do as we did as children — make a well in the middle of a pile of mashed potatoes and pour in a few spoonfuls of gravy.

Serves 8
PREPARATION TIME: 15 MINUTES
COOKING TIME: 1 HOUR 15 MINUTES

Ingredients:
4 TBSP GROUNDNUT OIL
1 KG NECK OR SCRAG END OF LAMB ON THE BONE, COARSELY CHOPPED
50G HONEY, PREFERABLY LAVENDER
100G CARROTS, COARSELY CHOPPED
100G ONIONS, COARSELY CHOPPED
200ML RED WINE
1.25L WATER
1 BOUQUET GARNI (PAGE 10)
6 PEPPERCORNS, CRUSHED
1 MARMANDE TOMATO, PEELED, DESEEDED AND CHOPPED
1 GARLIC CLOVE, CRUSHED
SALT AND FRESHLY GROUND PEPPER

Heat the oil in a deep frying pan, put in the lamb and fry briskly until browned all over. Pour off the oil and the fat released by the lamb. Using a palette knife, spread the honey over the pieces of lamb, then add the carrot and onion to the pan. Stir with a wooden spoon and sweat gently for 3 minutes. Deglaze with the red wine and cook over medium heat for 5 minutes. Add the rest of the ingredients, being sparing with the salt and pepper, and bubble the sauce gently for 1 hour, skimming the surface whenever necessary. Pass it through a conical sieve; it is now ready to serve, but for a more concentrated aroma, reduce the sauce for a little longer.

The sauce will keep in an airtight container in the fridge for a few days, or for several weeks in the freezer.

Orange Sauce

Sauce bigarade

I love this sauce served with slices of pan-fried calf's liver or sliced grilled kidneys. For a classic sauce for duck à l'orange, I add some duck wings (when I can get them), which I brown quickly before adding them to the sauce along with the veal stock at the beginning of cooking.

Serves 6
PREPARATION TIME: 10 MINUTES
COOKING TIME: ABOUT 50 MINUTES

Ingredients:
45G CASTER SUGAR
3 TBSP RED WINE VINEGAR
700ML VEAL STOCK (PAGE 16)
300G DUCK WINGS (OPTIONAL)
JUICE OF 3 ORANGES
JUICE OF 1 LEMON
ZEST OF 2 ORANGES, CUT INTO FINE JULIENNE AND BLANCHED
ZEST OF THE LEMON, CUT INTO FINE JULIENNE AND BLANCHED
SALT AND FRESHLY GROUND PEPPER

Put the sugar and vinegar in a deep frying pan and cook over a very low heat to make a deep golden caramel. Immediately pour in the veal stock and orange and lemon juice and bring to the boil. Lower the heat and cook gently for 45 minutes, skimming the surface whenever necessary. The sauce should now be thick enough to coat the back of a spoon lightly. If it is not, cook for a little longer. Pass the sauce through a conical sieve, season to taste with salt and pepper, then add the orange and lemon zests and serve. If you are not serving the sauce immediately, keep it warm in a bain-marie without adding the zests and add them only at the last moment.

Bordelaise Sauce

Sauce bordelaise

This wonderful sauce looks as good as it tastes. It is delectable with any cut of beef, such as entrecôte, ribs or sirloin. Personally, I add double the quantity of beef marrow, which I absolutely adore.

Serves 4
PREPARATION TIME: 10 MINUTES
COOKING TIME: ABOUT 30 MINUTES

Ingredients:
40G SHALLOTS, FINELY CHOPPED
8 WHITE PEPPERCORNS, CRUSHED
200ML CLARET
300ML VEAL STOCK (PAGE 16)
1 SMALL BOUQUET GARNI (PAGE 10)
200G BEEF MARROW, SOAKED IN ICED WATER FOR
4 HOURS
30G BUTTER, CHILLED AND DICED
SALT AND FRESHLY GROUND PEPPER

Put the shallot, crushed peppercorns and claret in a saucepan, set over high heat and reduce the wine by one-third. Add the veal stock and bouquet garni and bubble gently for about 20 minutes, or until the sauce will coat the back of a spoon. Pass it through a wire-mesh conical sieve into another saucepan.

Drain the beef marrow and cut it into small pieces or rounds. Place in a small saucepan, cover with a little cold water and salt lightly. Set over medium heat and bring to the boil. Immediately turn off the heat, leave the marrow for 30 seconds, then drain it carefully.

Season the sauce with salt and pepper to taste, whisk in the butter, add the well-drained beef marrow and serve immediately.

Aubergine Sauce with Tarragon

Sauce aubergine à l'estragon

The tarragon and mustard add a refreshing note to this sauce, while the aubergine makes it smooth and creamy. Serve it with roast rabbit, veal or pork chops. It also makes an excellent accompaniment to a dish of wide noodles.

Serves 4
PREPARATION TIME: 10 MINUTES
COOKING TIME: ABOUT 25 MINUTES

Ingredients:
2 TBSP OLIVE OIL
60G SHALLOTS, FINELY CHOPPED
150G AUBERGINE
50ML RED WINE
300ML VEAL STOCK (PAGE 16)
2 TBSP DOUBLE CREAM
A LARGE PINCH OF PAPRIKA
1 TBSP WHOLEGRAIN MUSTARD
1 TBSP SNIPPED TARRAGON
SALT

Cut the aubergine into cubes (do not peel it). Lightly salt the cubes, leave for 5 minutes to draw out any bitterness, then pat dry with kitchen paper. Heat the oil in a saucepan, then put in the shallot and cubes of aubergine. Cook over medium heat, stirring with a wooden spoon, until the aubergine begins to soften. Add the red wine and cook for 3 minutes, still over medium heat. Pour in the veal stock and bubble gently for 15 minutes. Add the cream and a generous pinch of paprika, then transfer the sauce to a blender and whizz for 30 seconds.

Pass the sauce through a wire-mesh conical sieve into another saucepan, add the mustard and tarragon and bring back to the boil. Season to taste with salt and serve at once.

Peach Sauce

Sauce aux pêches

I serve this delicate, fruity sauce with my pigeonneau de Bresse rôti aux pêches *or with a young duckling. For preference, make the sauce with white peaches.*

Serves 4
PREPARATION TIME: 10 MINUTES
COOKING TIME: ABOUT 45 MINUTES

Ingredients:
30G BUTTER
30G CASTER SUGAR
2 VERY RIPE MEDIUM PEACHES, PEELED AND CUT
INTO CUBES
20ML COGNAC
3 TBSP RED WINE VINEGAR
100ML RED WINE, PREFERABLY BURGUNDY
1 CLOVE
1 1/2 TSP FENNEL SEEDS
300ML VEAL STOCK (PAGE 16)
40G BUTTER, CHILLED AND DICED
SALT AND FRESHLY GROUND PEPPER

Melt the butter in a deep frying pan, add the sugar and stir with a wooden spoon. As soon as the sugar has caramelized and begun to colour lightly, put in the peach cubes and increase the heat. Cook, stirring continuously, until the peaches have almost collapsed into a purée. Add the Cognac, then, after 30 seconds, the vinegar. After 1 more minute, pour in the wine and add the clove and fennel seeds.

Bring to the boil and cook gently for 10 minutes, skimming the surface with a slotted spoon as necessary. Pour in the veal stock and cook the sauce for about 30 minutes, until it coats the back of a spoon. Pass it through a conical sieve, whisk in the butter, a little at a time, season to taste and serve immediately.

Zingara Sauce

Sauce zingara

Serve this fine, delicate sauce with pan-fried or grilled poultry or with veal escalopes, chops or scallopine.

Serves 6
PREPARATION TIME: 10 MINUTES
COOKING TIME: ABOUT 35 MINUTES

Ingredients:
400ML VEAL STOCK (PAGE 16)
1 TBSP COOKED TOMATO COULIS (PAGE 66)
30G BUTTER
60G BUTTON MUSHROOMS, CUT INTO BATONS
50ML DRY WHITE WINE
30G LEAN HAM, CUT INTO BATONS
30G COOKED OX TONGUE, CUT INTO BATONS
40G FRESH OR PRESERVED TRUFFLE, CUT INTO
BATONS
30ML BEST QUALITY MADEIRA
SALT AND CAYENNE PEPPER

Put the veal stock and tomato coulis in a saucepan, reduce by two-thirds over medium heat, then pass the liquid through a wire-mesh conical sieve into a bowl and set aside.

In another saucepan, melt the butter, add the mushrooms and sweat them gently for 30 seconds. Pour in the white wine and reduce it almost completely. Add the ham, tongue and truffle, mix delicately with a wooden spoon, then pour in the Madeira and cook at a bare simmer for 2 minutes. Add the reduced veal stock and simmer for another 5 minutes. Season the sauce to taste with salt and cayenne and serve at once.

Exotic Sauce

Sauce exotique

This fruity, refreshing sauce has a light spiciness. It is particularly good with sautéed chicken or rabbit, accompanied by some leaf spinach or fresh pasta.

Serves 4
PREPARATION TIME: 5 MINUTES
COOKING TIME: ABOUT 15 MINUTES

Ingredients:
1 VERY RIPE MANGO
2 PASSION FRUIT
2 TBSP COGNAC OR ARMAGNAC
200ML VEAL STOCK (PAGE 16)
100ML DOUBLE CREAM
4 DROPS OF TABASCO
SALT AND FRESHLY GROUND PEPPER

Using a small knife with a flexible blade, peel the mango and cut off the flesh around the stone. Finely dice the flesh and place in a small saucepan. Halve the passion fruit, scoop the seeds into the saucepan and add the Cognac or Armagnac. Cook the exotic fruit mixture over low heat for 5 minutes, then add the veal stock and cook for another 5 minutes. Pour in the cream, add the Tabasco and bubble the sauce for 5 minutes, then transfer to a blender and whizz for 1 minute. Pass the sauce through a wire-mesh conical sieve into a small saucepan, season to taste with salt and pepper and serve immediately, or keep it warm for a few minutes in a bain-marie.

PEEL THE MANGO AND CUT OFF THE FLESH AROUND THE STONE

HALVE THE PASSION FRUIT AND SCOOP OUT THE SEEDS

ADD THE COLD VEAL STOCK

ADD THE TABASCO

PURÉE THE SAUCE IN A BLENDER

Juniper Sauce

Sauce au genièvre

This sauce is simple but highly scented, with a hint of muskiness. It is perfect with grilled or pan-fried steaks or lightly cooked game, such as pan-fried fillets of hare or medallions of venison.

Serves 6
PREPARATION TIME: 5 MINUTES
COOKING TIME: ABOUT 25 MINUTES

Ingredients:
40G SHALLOTS, CHOPPED
200ML RED WINE, PREFERABLY CÔTES DU RHÔNE
300ML VEAL STOCK (PAGE 16)
14 JUNIPER BERRIES, CRUSHED
2 TBSP REDCURRANT JELLY
40G BUTTER, CHILLED AND DICED
SALT AND FRESHLY GROUND PEPPER

Put the shallot and wine in a saucepan, set over medium heat and reduce the wine by one-third. Add the veal stock, then the juniper berries and bubble gently for 15 minutes. Stir in the redcurrant jelly and, as soon as it has dissolved, pass the sauce through a wire-mesh conical sieve into a clean pan. Whisk in the butter, a little at a time, season to taste with salt and pepper and serve immediately.

Bolognaise Sauce

Sauce bolognaise

I love this sauce served with a good thick potato purée, braised white cabbage, pan-fried turkey escalopes and, of course, its classic partner, spaghetti.

Serves 8
PREPARATION TIME: 10 MINUTES
COOKING TIME: ABOUT 40 MINUTES

Ingredients:
50ML GROUNDNUT OIL
400G BEEF OR LAMB, FRESHLY MINCED
80G ONIONS, CHOPPED
1 MEDIUM GARLIC CLOVE, FINELY CHOPPED
1 SMALL BOUQUET GARNI (PAGE 10), INCLUDING A SPRIG OF ROSEMARY
300ML COOKED TOMATO COULIS (PAGE 66)
300ML VEAL STOCK (PAGE 16)
40G BUTTER, CHILLED AND DICED
1 TBSP CHOPPED PARSLEY
SALT AND FRESHLY GROUND PEPPER

In a frying pan, heat 40ml of the oil and, when it is very hot, add the minced meat and seal and brown it all over, stirring with a wooden spoon. Immediately tip it into a colander and leave for 30 seconds to drain off the cooking fat.

Put the remaining oil in a saucepan, add the onions and sweat them gently for 30 seconds without colouring. Add the meat, garlic, bouquet garni, tomato coulis and veal stock and bring to the boil. Immediately lower the heat and simmer the sauce gently for 35 minutes, stirring every 5–10 minutes with a wooden spoon. Remove the bouquet garni and beat the butter into the sauce with the wooden spoon, a little at a time. Season with salt and plenty of pepper and stir in the parsley just before serving.

Devil Sauce

Sauce diable

I often use this robust, highly scented sauce, which goes very well with all grilled poultry, particularly spatchcocked poussin or chicken.

Serves 4
PREPARATION TIME: 5 MINUTES
COOKING TIME: ABOUT 45 MINUTES

Ingredients:
30ML BEST QUALITY RED WINE VINEGAR
100ML DRY WHITE WINE
20 WHITE PEPPERCORNS, CRUSHED
50G SHALLOTS, CHOPPED
I BOUQUET GARNI (PAGE 10),
INCLUDING 2 SPRIGS OF TARRAGON
400ML VEAL STOCK (PAGE 16)
40G BUTTER, CHILLED AND DICED
I TBSP SNIPPED CHERVIL OR FLAT-LEAF PARSLEY
SALT AND FRESHLY GROUND PEPPER

Combine the vinegar, white wine, crushed white peppercorns, shallot and bouquet garni in a saucepan. Set over medium heat and reduce the liquid by four-fifths. Pour in the veal stock and bubble gently for about 20 minutes, or until the sauce is thick enough to coat the back of a spoon. Pass it through a wire-mesh sieve into a clean saucepan and whisk in the butter, a little at a time. Season to taste with salt and pepper and add the chervil or parsley just before serving.

Light Chicken Sauce with Curaçao

Sauce volaille au Curaçao

This sauce has a very light consistency, almost like a thin gravy. I like to serve it with roast or pan-fried poussin or pigeon. You can accentuate the Curaçao flavour by adding a touch more of the liqueur.

Serves 4
PREPARATION TIME: 5 MINUTES
COOKING TIME: ABOUT 30 MINUTES

Ingredients:
2 TBSP GROUNDNUT OIL
250G CHICKEN WINGS AND NECKS, BLANCHED,
REFRESHED AND DRAINED
60G SHALLOTS, DICED
80G CARROTS, DICED
60G CELERY, DICED
4 STAR ANISE, COARSELY CHOPPED
30ML CURAÇAO
200ML CHICKEN STOCK (PAGE 18)
200ML VEAL STOCK (PAGE 16)
30G BUTTER, CHILLED AND DICED
SALT AND FRESHLY GROUND PEPPER

Heat the oil in a deep frying pan, put in the chicken wings and necks and quickly brown them all over. Pour off the oil and fat rendered by the chicken, then add the diced vegetables to the chicken in the pan, together with the star anise and sweat everything gently for 2 minutes.

Add the Curaçao, cook for 1 minute, then pour in the chicken stock, increase the heat to high and reduce the stock by half. Add the veal stock and simmer the sauce gently for another 20 minutes. Pass it through a wire-mesh conical sieve into a clean pan, whisk in the butter a little at a time, season to taste with salt and pepper and serve immediately.

Cherry Tomato Sauce

Sauce aux petites tomates cerises

This sauce is delicious served not only with pasta, but also with many grilled white meats. I greedily sup it with a spoon. It can be reheated very successfully and will keep in an airtight container in the fridge for several days.

Serves 8
PREPARATION TIME: 15 MINUTES
COOKING TIME: ABOUT 1 HOUR

Ingredients:
1 KG VERY RIPE CHERRY TOMATOES, STALKS
REMOVED
1 TSP CASTER SUGAR
1 TBSP SNIPPED BASIL LEAVES
30ML RUBY PORT
3 TBSP OLIVE OIL
60G ONIONS, CHOPPED
80G CELERY, CHOPPED
6 THICK SLICES OF BACON (ABOUT 120G),
DE-RINDED AND DICED
6 DROPS OF TABASCO
1 TSP WORCESTERSHIRE SAUCE
JUICE OF 1/2 LEMON
SALT AND FRESHLY GROUND PEPPER

Preheat the oven to 160°C/320°F/gas mark 3.

Put the tomatoes into an ovenproof earthenware or enamel casserole with a lid and add the sugar, basil, port and a little salt. Cover and cook in the oven for about 45 minutes, until the tomatoes have collapsed into a purée.

Meanwhile, combine the olive oil, onion, celery and bacon in a saucepan and set over medium heat. Cook for about 20 minutes, stirring frequently with a wooden spoon, until everything is pale golden and well softened. Spoon off the excess oil, then mix the contents of the saucepan with the tomatoes. Transfer to a blender and whizz for 1 minute. Pass the sauce through a wire-mesh conical sieve into another saucepan and add the Tabasco, Worcestershire sauce, lemon juice and salt and pepper to taste. Simmer the sauce for another 5 minutes, then serve immediately.

Savory and Tapenade Sauce

Sauce sarriette et tapenade

This sauce is very fluid, almost like a jus, and bursting with the Provençal flavours of savory and olives. I often serve it with pan-fried or roast saddle, shoulder or leg of lamb. If you happen to have some lamb stock, substitute it for the veal stock.

Serves 4
PREPARATION TIME: 5 MINUTES
COOKING TIME: ABOUT 25 MINUTES

Ingredients:
100ML DRY WHITE WINE
40G SHALLOT, CHOPPED
15G SAVORY
6 WHITE PEPPERCORNS, CRUSHED
200ML VEAL STOCK (PAGE 16)
60G BLACK OR GREEN TAPENADE (OLIVE PASTE)
30G BUTTER, CHILLED AND DICED
SALT AND FRESHLY GROUND PEPPER

Combine the wine, shallot, savory and crushed peppercorns in a small saucepan, set over medium heat and reduce the wine by half. Pour in the veal stock, reduce the heat to very low and simmer gently for 20 minutes. Whisk in the tapenade, then, still over the lowest possible heat, whisk in the butter, a little at a time. Season the sauce with salt and pepper, pass it through a wire-mesh conical sieve and serve at once.

Curry Sauce

Sauce au curry

Serve this creamy, slightly fruity sauce with simply grilled veal escalopes or chicken, garnished with curried or pilaff rice. The quantity of curry powder can be varied to suit your own taste.

Serves 8
PREPARATION TIME: 10 MINUTES
COOKING TIME: ABOUT 30 MINUTES

Ingredients:
40G BUTTER
60G ONIONS, CHOPPED
300G PINEAPPLE, CUT INTO SMALL PIECES
1 MEDIUM BANANA, CUT INTO ROUNDS
1 DESSERT APPLE (PREFERABLY A COX), WASHED AND
CUT INTO SMALL PIECES
40G CURRY POWDER
2 TBSP GRATED FRESH OR DESICCATED COCONUT
300ML VEAL STOCK (PAGE 16)
200ML COCONUT MILK
SALT

Melt the butter in a saucepan, add the onions and sweat them over low heat for 1 minute. Add the pineapple, banana and apple and cook gently for 5 minutes, stirring with a wooden spoon. Add the curry and grated coconut, then pour in the veal stock and coconut milk. Bring to the boil and bubble the sauce gently for 20 minutes. Pass it through a wire-mesh conical sieve, season with salt to taste and serve immediately. If you wish, you can keep the sauce warm in a bain-marie; dot the surface with a few flakes of butter to prevent a skin from forming.

Five-spice Sauce

Sauce aux cinq épices

This sauce is excellent with a chicken baked in a salt crust, or with pan-fried veal tournedos served with pilaff rice.

Serves 4
PREPARATION TIME: 20 MINUTES
COOKING TIME: ABOUT 30 MINUTES

Ingredients:
250G CHICKEN WINGS, BLANCHED,
REFRESHED AND DRAINED
2 TBSP GROUNDNUT OIL
60G CARROTS, CHOPPED
60G ONIONS, CHOPPED
50ML WHITE WINE VINEGAR
400ML CHICKEN STOCK (PAGE 18)
80G TOMATOES, PEELED, DESEEDED
AND CHOPPED
1 SMALL BOUQUET GARNI (PAGE 10),
INCLUDING A SPRIG OF TARRAGON
100ML DOUBLE CREAM
1 TSP FIVE-SPICE POWDER
SALT AND FRESHLY GROUND PEPPER

Put the chicken wings and oil in a deep frying pan and brown over high heat. Pour off the oil and fat from the chicken, then add the carrots and onions to the pan and sweat them for 2 minutes. Off the heat, sprinkle on the vinegar and leave for 1 minute. Add the chicken stock, tomatoes and bouquet garni, bring to the boil, then cook over low heat, skimming the surface whenever necessary, until the sauce lightly coats the back of a spoon. Add the cream and five-spice powder and bubble gently for 2 minutes. Pass the sauce through a wire-mesh conical sieve and season to taste. Keep it warm in a bain-marie or serve immediately.

ADD THE ONIONS AND
CARROTS TO THE PAN

SPRINKLE IN THE VINEGAR

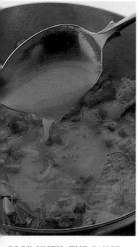

COOK UNTIL THE SAUCE
LIGHTLY COATS THE BACK
OF THE SPOON

ADD THE FIVE-SPICE POWDER

Choose the sauce for a dessert according to the main ingredient. As with savoury dishes, the purpose of the sauce is to accompany the principle ingredient but never to dominate it. Remember that the dessert comes at the end of the meal; being the last dish, it creates the final and lasting impression, so it must be perfect.

Dessert Sauces

The star of this chapter is crème anglaise, the most famous, classic and well-loved sweet sauce, which sadly is also one of the most ill-used and badly-executed. Crème anglaise should be like a perfect hollandaise — creamy, unctuous, rich yet delicate, with a superb mouth feel; then I adore it, supping it up with a spoon like soup. But when it is watery, insipid and depressingly unsatisfying on the palate, I cannot swallow it. This is why I have made my recipe as explicit as possible, by means of clear step-by-step photographic instructions. Apart from the classic addition of vanilla, the sauce can be scented with many other flavourings to make it shine like a beacon.

Fruit coulis are deliciously refreshing, with bright glowing colours and flavours ranging from sweet to bitter or acid, depending on the fruit used. They can be enhanced with a touch of spices. Stored in airtight containers, they will keep very well in the fridge for several days.

Bear in mind that you should never serve more than one or two coulis on the same plate with fruits or a dessert. Each one has its own distinctive flavour which could be diametrically opposed to another. To maintain the harmony of flavours and aromas, avoid the temptation to combine a riot of different colours on the plate; this will only spoil your dessert.

Chocolate sauces should be served at the right temperature (between 30° and 40°C) and made with the finest quality chocolate for the best results.

Many dessert sauces and coulis are delicious served with ice creams and sorbets. What could be more divine than vanilla or pistachio ice cream coated with warm chocolate sauce?

POACHED PEARS WITH
BLACKBERRY COULIS

Stock Syrup

Sirop à sorbet ou coulis de fruits

This basic syrup (30° on the Beaumé scale or 1.2624 density) is used with fresh fruits to make fruit sorbets and coulis which can accompany any number of desserts.

Makes about 700ml
PREPARATION TIME: 5 MINUTES
COOKING TIME: ABOUT 7 MINUTES

Ingredients:
400G CASTER SUGAR
350ML COLD WATER
50G LIQUID GLUCOSE

Combine the sugar, water and glucose in a saucepan and bring slowly to the boil over low heat, stirring continuously with a wooden spoon. Boil for 3 minutes, skimming the surface if necessary. Pass the syrup through a wire-mesh conical sieve and leave to cool before refrigerating.

Stock syrup will keep in an airtight container in the fridge for up to 2 weeks.

Blackberry Coulis

Coulis de mûres

This divine coulis can accompany almost all charlottes, whatever their flavour. It is equally delicious served with parfaits or iced bombes, or ice creams such as coconut, vanilla or banana. Like all coulis, it will keep well for several days in an airtight container in the fridge.

Serves 8
PREPARATION TIME: 5 MINUTES

Ingredients:
350G RIPE BLACKBERRIES, HULLED
50ML KIRSCH
150ML STOCK SYRUP (LEFT)
JUICE OF 1/2 LEMON

Put all the ingredients in a blender and whizz for about 1 minute, until puréed. Rub the sauce through a wire-mesh conical sieve and serve cold.

(Picture page 156)

Grapefruit Coulis with Mint

Coulis de pamplemousse à la menthe

This refreshing coulis marries well with orange desserts, chocolate charlotte or blackcurrant sorbet. It looks very attractive if you scatter over a few mint leaves snipped as finely as possible just before serving.

Serves 6
PREPARATION TIME: 5 MINUTES

Ingredients:
2 GRAPEFRUIT, PREFERABLY PINK, EACH ABOUT 400G
10G FRESH MINT, SNIPPED
40G CASTER SUGAR
150G PLAIN YOGHURT
25ML VODKA

Using a knife with a flexible blade, peel the grapefruit, removing all pith and membrane and cut each one into six. Place in a blender with the mint and sugar, whizz for 1 minute and pass through a wire-mesh conical sieve into a mixing bowl. Whisk in the yoghurt, then mix in the vodka. Serve very cold.

Coulis of Pears with Red Wine

Coulis de poires au vin rouge

Serve this powerful and delicious coulis with an iced vacherin, a Saint-Honoré filled with whipped cream with an accompaniment of red berries, or with a simple compote of fresh apricots. The coulis will keep well for several days in an airtight container in the fridge.

Serves 6
PREPARATION TIME: 10 MINUTES,
PLUS 30 MINUTES' MARINATING

Ingredients:
3 VERY RIPE PEARS, EACH ABOUT 200G
A PINCH OF GROUND CINNAMON
100ML RED WINE, PREFERABLY CLARET
30ML COLD WATER
JUICE OF $1/2$ LEMON
150G CASTER SUGAR

Peel and core the pears. Cut them into small pieces and place in a bowl with the cinnamon and red wine. Cover with cling film and leave to marinate for 30 minutes.

Combine the water, lemon juice and sugar in a thick-bottomed saucepan. Heat the mixture over very low heat and bubble it gently until it becomes a pale caramel. Take the pan off the heat and pour in the red wine in which you marinated the pears. (Be careful not to get splashed as the cold wine hits the hot caramel). After 5 minutes, stir the diluted and cooled caramel with a wooden spoon, then pour it over the pears. Transfer to a blender and whizz for 1 minute, then chill the coulis before serving. If it becomes too thick, dilute it with 2 or 3 spoons of cold water.

TOP RIGHT:
WARM PLUM TART WITH
ORANGE BUTTER

Orange Butter

Beurre à l'orange

This is delicious served with crêpes, lemon charlotte, a warm plum tart or a chocolate soufflé. A few drops of Grand Marnier or Curaçao add extra warmth to the sauce in winter.

Serves 6
PREPARATION TIME: 5 MINUTES
COOKING TIME: ABOUT 5 MINUTES

Ingredients:
JUICE OF 6 ORANGES, EACH ABOUT 250G, STRAINED
THROUGH A CONICAL SIEVE
100G ICING SUGAR
125G BUTTER, SOFTENED TO A PASTE

Put the orange juice and sugar in a saucepan and reduce by half over medium heat. Turn off the heat and whisk in the softened butter, a little at a time. Serve the sauce at room temperature.

Crème Anglaise

Crème anglaise (custard sauce) can accompany any number of cold desserts. For a light, foamy, unctuous sauce to serve with a hot dessert like apple charlotte, warm rice pudding or chocolate soufflé, warm the custard slightly and add a little Grand Marnier, Champagne or other alcohol, then whizz it in a blender for 30 seconds. Crème anglaise can also be churned to make the ever-popular vanilla ice cream.

Makes about 750ml
PREPARATION TIME: 15 MINUTES
COOKING TIME: ABOUT 5 MINUTES

Ingredients:
6 EGG YOLKS
125G CASTER SUGAR
500ML MILK
1 VANILLA POD, SPLIT LENGTHWAYS

ADD MELTED CHOCOLATE
FOR A CHOCOLATE CRÈME
ANGLAISE

In a bowl, whisk the egg yolks with one-third of the sugar (1) until the mixture is pale and has a ribbon consistency (2). Put the milk, vanilla and the remaining sugar in a saucepan (3), stir with a whisk for a few seconds, then bring to the boil. Pour the boiling milk on to the egg yolks, whisking continuously (4). Return the mixture to the pan and cook gently, stirring with a wooden spoon, until the temperature of the custard reaches about 80°C. It should have thickened enough to coat the back of the wooden spoon and for your finger to leave a trail when you run it down the spoon.

Remove the vanilla pod and immediately pour the sauce into a clean bowl set in crushed ice to speed up the cooling process. Stir the custard occasionally with a wooden spoon to stop it from coagulating and prevent a skin from forming. Once it is completely cold, cover with cling film and refrigerate for a minimum of 2 and a maximum of 48 hours.

THE CUSTARD SAUCE
SHOULD COAT THE
BACK OF A SPOON

COFFEE OR CHOCOLATE CRÈME ANGLAISE:
For a coffee or chocolate crème anglaise, replace the vanilla with 2tbsp instant coffee powder or 60g melted bitter chocolate.

CHECK THE CONSISTENCY OF
THE CUSTARD SAUCE ON THE
BACK OF A WOODEN SPOON

Liquorice Sauce

Sauce à la réglisse

This unusual sauce has a delicious flavour of liquorice, which perfectly complements a pear tart, mirabelle clafoutis, pistachio ice cream or a compote of yellow peaches.

I add whipped cream just before serving to lighten and soften the sauce. Without the addition of the cream, it will keep well in the fridge for 48 hours, covered with cling film.

Serves 6
PREPARATION TIME: 15 MINUTES
COOKING TIME: ABOUT 5 MINUTES

Ingredients:
3 EGG YOLKS
60G CASTER SUGAR
250ML MILK
25G LIQUORICE EXTRACT, OR 50G LIQUORICE STICKS, CUT INTO SMALL PIECES
50ML WHIPPING CREAM, WHIPPED UNTIL FLOPPY

Follow the method for crème anglaise (page 161), substituting the liquorice for the vanilla. Add the whipped cream just before serving.

Autumnal Sauce

Sauce automnale

This autumnal sauce is lovely with a compote of peaches or figs, or with baked apples.

Serves 8
PREPARATION TIME: 5 MINUTES
COOKING TIME: 10 MINUTES

Ingredients:
1 DESSERT APPLE, ABOUT 100G
2 MEDIUM BANANAS
JUICE OF 1 LEMON
50G HONEY
SEEDS FROM 2 CARDAMOM PODS
100G CASTER SUGAR
200ML WATER

Peel and core the apple and dice it finely. Peel the bananas and cut them into rounds.

Put the prepared fruits in a saucepan with the lemon juice, honey, cardamom seeds, sugar and water and bring to the boil over low heat. Simmer very gently for 10 minutes, then pour into a blender and purée for 1 minute, or until very smooth. Pass the sauce through a conical sieve into a bowl, leave at room temperature until cold, then refrigerate until ready to use.

Strawberry Coulis with Green Peppercorns

Coulis de fraises au poivre vert

I usually serve this coulis poured around a lemon sorbet, vanilla ice cream, or perhaps a poached pear or pear charlotte. Occasionally in summer I make amuse-gueules of thinly-sliced marinated raw tuna encircled by a ribbon of this refreshing sauce.

Serves 8
PREPARATION TIME: 5 MINUTES

Ingredients:
500G VERY RIPE STRAWBERRIES, HULLED
10G SOFT GREEN BOTTLED PEPPERCORNS, WELL DRAINED
100ML STOCK SYRUP (PAGE 158)
JUICE OF 1/2 LEMON
10G POPPY SEEDS (OPTIONAL)

Put the strawberries, peppercorns, syrup and lemon juice in a blender and whizz for 1 minute. Pass the coulis through a wire-mesh conical sieve and, if you wish, add the poppy seeds just before serving.

PUT THE STRAWBERRIES,
PEPPERCORNS, SYRUP AND LEMON
JUICE INTO A BLENDER

RIGHT AND ABOVE: WHIZZ TO A
PURÉE FOR ABOUT 1 MINUTE

PASS THE COULIS THROUGH A
WIRE-MESH CONICAL SIEVE

ADD THE COFFEE TO THE
MAPLE SYRUP

WHISK IN THE ALCOHOL

Maple Syrup, Coffee and Drambuie Sauce

Sauce café et Drambuie

This limpid, iridescent sauce is delicious served with a vanilla and praline parfait *or with warm waffles. The alcohol adds an agreeable aroma, which is especially attractive in winter.*

Serves 6
PREPARATION TIME: 5 MINUTES
COOKING TIME: ABOUT 2 MINUTES

Ingredients:
200ML MAPLE SYRUP
1 TBSP INSTANT COFFEE, DISSOLVED
IN 1 TBSP WATER
50ML VODKA
50ML DRAMBUIE
8 COFFEE BEANS, COARSELY CRUSHED

In a small saucepan, warm the maple syrup, then add the coffee. As soon as the syrup is hot but not boiling, take the pan off the heat and whisk in the vodka and Drambuie, not too vigorously. Cover the sauce with cling film and keep in a cool place until cold. Stir in the crushed coffee beans just before serving.

WARM WAFFLES WITH
MAPLE SYRUP, COFFEE AND
DRAMBUIE SAUCE

Prune and Armagnac Sauce

Sauce aux pruneaux et à l'Armagnac

This sauce is ideal in autumn, served with moulded rice pudding, a hot soufflé of marrons glacés, pear or banana ice cream and, of course, a prune clafoutis.

Serves 10
PREPARATION TIME: 10 MINUTES
COOKING TIME: ABOUT 30 MINUTES

Ingredients:
250G PRUNES, PREFERABLY AGEN, SOAKED IN COLD
WATER FOR 6 HOURS
150G CASTER SUGAR
1/2 CINNAMON STICK
150ML ARMAGNAC
250G BUTTER

Drain the soaked prunes, place them in a saucepan with the sugar and cinnamon and cover with cold water. Bring slowly to the boil over low heat and simmer for 20 minutes. Transfer to a bowl, remove the cinnamon and leave the prunes to cool, then drain and stone them. Reserve the cooking syrup.

Cut six of the prunes into small, even pieces and reserve them in a bowl. Put the remaining prunes in a shallow pan with the Armagnac, 150ml cooking syrup from the prunes and 100g butter and heat gently without boiling to about 60–70°C. Transfer to a blender and whizz for 1 minute. Scrape the puréed prunes into a saucepan and whisk in the remaining butter, a small piece at a time, and enough of the reserved syrup to give the sauce a light ribbon consistency. Add the prune pieces and serve the sauce tepid, or keep it in a bain-marie filled with not-too-hot water for a maximum of 30 minutes.

SIMMER THE HALVED PEACHES IN
THE SYRUP FOR 20 MINUTES

PURÉE THE PEACHES FOR 2
MINUTES TO MAKE A COULIS

White Peach Coulis with Star Anise

Coulis de pêches blanches à l'anis étoilé

This coulis is the perfect accompaniment for white peaches, either raw or lightly poached in syrup and served cold or warm. It is also excellent with wild strawberries or any delicate fruits.

Serves 8
PREPARATION TIME: 10 MINUTES
COOKING TIME: ABOUT 20 MINUTES

Ingredients:
2 VERY RIPE WHITE PEACHES
400ML WATER
150G CASTER SUGAR
4 STAR ANISE AND 2 CLOVES, TIED UP TOGETHER IN
A SQUARE OF MUSLIN
JUICE OF 1 LEMON
2 ORANGES, PREFERABLY BLOOD ORANGES
1 TBSP GRENADINE SYRUP (IF YOU ARE NOT USING
BLOOD ORANGES)

Put the peaches in a bowl, cover with boiling water and leave for 15 seconds, then transfer to a bowl of cold water, using a slotted spoon. Skin and halve them with a sharp knife, leaving in the stones.

Place the halved peaches with their stones in a small saucepan. Add the water, sugar, star anise, cloves and lemon juice, set over low heat and bring to just below boiling point. Simmer for 20 minutes, then leave to cool at room temperature for 15 minutes.

Discard the peach stones and spices. Purée the contents of the pan in a blender for about 2 minutes, to make a coulis. Pass this through a fine-mesh conical strainer and keep in a cool place.

To make the orange syrup, squeeze the oranges and strain the juice into a small saucepan. Add the grenadine and reduce the juice over low heat until it becomes syrupy. Reserve it in a ramekin.

Pour the peach coulis around the fruits on individual plates and spoon a ribbon of orange syrup on to it. Using a cocktail stick or the tip of a knife, delicately swirl the syrup into the coulis.

RIGHT: SKIN THE
PEACHES BY POURING
ON BOILING WATER

SWIRL THE ORANGE SYRUP
INTO THE PEACH COULIS

TOSS THE SLICED BANANAS IN
LEMON JUICE

Honey Sauce

Sauce au miel

*This ambrosial sauce, lightly perfumed with honey, is delicious
with pancakes, crisp apple tartlets, French toast and ice cream.*

Serves 8
PREPARATION TIME: 5 MINUTES
COOKING TIME: ABOUT 10 MINUTES

Ingredients:
200G RIPE BANANAS (PEELED WEIGHT)
JUICE OF 1 LEMON
300ML STOCK SYRUP (PAGE 158)
5G GROUND GINGER
60G HONEY

Cut the bananas into rounds and immediately toss
them in the lemon juice. Put them in a saucepan with
the syrup, ginger and honey and boil for 5 minutes.
Transfer to a blender and whizz for 1 minute, then pass
the sauce through a wire-mesh conical sieve into a
bowl. Stir until cold, cover with cling film and
refrigerate until ready to use.

PASS THE SAUCE
THROUGH A
WIRE-MESH
CONICAL SIEVE

PUT THEM IN A PAN WITH THE
SYRUP, GINGER AND HONEY

Coffee Sabayon with Tia Maria

Sabayon au café Tia Maria

This sabayon *is really a dessert in itself, but it also makes a delicious sauce for such puddings as* gâteau de riz impératrice, *apple flan or pears poached in syrup.*

Serves 4
PREPARATION TIME: 15–20 MINUTES
COOKING TIME: 15–20 MINUTES

Ingredients:
50ML COLD WATER
2 TBSP INSTANT COFFEE
50G CASTER SUGAR
4 EGG YOLKS
50ML TIA MARIA

Half-fill with warm water a saucepan large enough to hold the base of a mixing bowl. Combine the cold water and coffee in the said bowl and whisk with a balloon whisk to dissolve the coffee. Still whisking, add all the other ingredients.

Stand the base of the bowl in the saucepan of water and set the pan over medium heat. Start whisking and continue to do so for 10–12 minutes. The temperature of the water in the saucepan must not exceed 90°C, or the *sabayon* will start to coagulate. It is ready when it reaches the consistency of egg whites beaten to soft peaks, with an unctuous, shiny, fluffy and light texture and a temperature not exceeding 55°C. As soon as the *sabayon* is ready, stop whisking, spoon it into bowls, large glasses or a sauceboat and serve immediately.

Mint Sauce

Sauce à la menthe

This creamy, refreshing sauce is excellent served with orange and grapefruit segments or a gâteau fraisier, or as a substitute for crème anglaise to accompany floating islands.

Serves 4
PREPARATION TIME: 15 MINUTES
COOKING TIME: ABOUT 5 MINUTES

Ingredients:
250ML MILK
75G CASTER SUGAR
40G FRESH MINT
3 EGG YOLKS
1 TBSP SNIPPED MINT LEAVES
A FEW DROPS OF GREEN PEPPERMINT SYRUP

Put the milk and two-thirds of the sugar into a saucepan and bring slowly to the boil over low heat. As soon as it boils, turn off the heat, add the 40g mint, cover and leave to infuse for 10 minutes.

Put the egg yolks and remaining sugar in a bowl and whisk to a foamy ribbon consistency. Pour the milk infusion on to the egg mixture, stirring all the time. Return the mixture to the saucepan and cook gently over low heat, stirring continuously, until the temperature of the custard reaches about 80°C and it is thick enough to coat the back of a spoon. Run your finger down the spoon; it should leave a clear trail. Immediately pass the sauce through a wire-mesh conical sieve into a clean bowl. Leave to cool at room temperature, stirring occasionally to stop the sauce coagulating and a skin from forming.

Cover the cold sauce with cling film and refrigerate for up to 48 hours. Just before serving, add the snipped mint and a few drops of green mint syrup.

Caramel Sauce

Sauce caramel

This simple, delicious sauce can be served with a multitude of desserts, and can even be stirred into yoghurt. It will keep well in an airtight container in the fridge for several days.

Serves 6
PREPARATION TIME: 5 MINUTES
COOKING TIME: ABOUT 15 MINUTES

Ingredients:
100G CASTER SUGAR
75G BUTTER, SOFTENED
1 VANILLA POD, SPLIT LENGTHWAYS AND SEEDS
SCRAPED OUT WITH THE TIP OF A KNIFE
400ML DOUBLE CREAM

In a thick-bottomed saucepan, combine the sugar, butter and the seeds from the vanilla pod. Set over very low heat and stir continuously with a wooden spoon until the sugar has dissolved completely. Continue to cook until the mixture turns an attractive caramel colour. Immediately, take the pan off the heat and stir in the cream, taking care that you are not spattered as the cold cream hits the hot caramel. Mix well and cook the sauce over medium heat for 5 minutes, stirring continuously with the wooden spoon. The sauce should be perfectly blended, pliable and shiny. Pass it through a wire-mesh conical sieve and leave to cool at room temperature before serving.

Rum Sauce

Sauce au rhum

The perfect complement to bread and butter pudding, Christmas pudding and rum and raisin ice cream.

Serves 6
PREPARATION TIME: 5 MINUTES
COOKING TIME: ABOUT 10 MINUTES

Ingredients:
300ML DOUBLE CREAM
60G CASTER SUGAR
2 TSP CORNFLOUR, SLAKED IN 2 TBSP MILK
75ML DARK RUM (PREFERABLY CAPTAIN MORGAN
OR NEGRITA)
20G SULTANAS, BLANCHED, REFRESHED
AND DRAINED

Put the cream and sugar in a small saucepan and bring to the boil over low heat. Add the slaked cornflour, stirring as you go, bubble for 2 minutes, then pour in the rum. Simmer the sauce for another 2 minutes, stir in the sultanas and serve piping hot.

Light Chocolate Sauce

Sauce au chocolat légère

This light sauce has a good bitter chocolate flavour. It is easy to prepare and is satisfyingly low in calories. Serve it in ladlefuls with profiteroles, ice creams and pear desserts.

Serves 6
PREPARATION TIME: 10 MINUTES
COOKING TIME: ABOUT 5 MINUTES

Ingredients:
100G UNSWEETENED COCOA POWDER
150G CASTER SUGAR
350ML WATER
20G BUTTER, SOFTENED

Combine the cocoa, sugar and water in a saucepan and whisk until well amalgamated. Bring to the boil over low heat, whisking continuously, and boil for 2 minutes. Whisk in the butter, a little at a time and cook for another 2 minutes. Serve the sauce immediately or keep it warm in a bain-marie for a few minutes.

Rich Chocolate Sauce

Sauce au chocolat riche

This rich, velvety sauce is ideal spooned over vanilla or coffee ice cream or meringues filled with whipped cream. Memories of childhood....

Serves 6
PREPARATION TIME: 10 MINUTES
COOKING TIME: ABOUT 5 MINUTES

Ingredients:
200G BEST QUALITY BITTER CHOCOLATE OR
COUVERTURE, CHOPPED
150ML MILK
2 TBSP DOUBLE CREAM
30G CASTER SUGAR
30G BUTTER, DICED

Put the chocolate in a bowl and gently melt it over a pan of simmering water, stirring with a wooden spoon until very smooth. Combine the milk, cream and sugar in a saucepan, stir with a whisk and bring to the boil. Still stirring, pour the boiling milk mixture on to the melted chocolate, then return the mixture to the pan and bubble it for a few seconds, stirring continuously. Turn off the heat and add the butter, a little at a time, whisking until the sauce is smooth and homogeneous. Pass it through a wire-mesh conical sieve and serve hot.

White Chocolate Sauce with Mint

Sauce au chocolat blanc et à la menthe

The mint adds freshness to this sauce, which is ideal for making a marriage of two chocolate sauces with a selection of all-chocolate desserts. It is also delicious served over dark chocolate ice cream with a few pistachios scattered on top.

Serves 6
PREPARATION TIME: 10 MINUTES
COOKING TIME: ABOUT 5 MINUTES

Ingredients:
250G WHITE COUVERTURE OR BEST QUALITY WHITE
CHOCOLATE, CHOPPED
100ML MILK
250ML DOUBLE CREAM
7G FRESH MINT LEAVES
3/4 TSP CARAWAY SEEDS

Put the white chocolate in a bowl, stand it in a bain-marie and melt it gently over low heat, stirring with a wooden spoon until smooth.

In a saucepan, bring the milk and cream to the boil. As soon as it begins to bubble, toss in the mint leaves and caraway seeds, turn off the heat and cover the pan. Leave to infuse for 10 minutes, then pass the milk mixture through a wire-mesh conical sieve on to the melted chocolate. Mix with a whisk until thoroughly amalgamated.

Transfer the chocolate sauce to a clean saucepan, set over medium heat and bubble for a few seconds, whisking continuously. Serve the sauce hot. If you are not serving it immediately, you can keep it warm in a bain-marie for a few minutes.

Matching sauces with ingredients

In this section you will find sauces designed to match whichever main ingredient you already have in your larder or fridge, or which takes your fancy when you do your food shopping. Now you need no longer wonder how to add interest to vegetables, pasta, fish, meat or fruit – just consult this index; you will find the perfect partner for whatever you plan to cook.

Index

Page numbers in *italic* refer to the illustrations